Backpacking with Small Children

BACKPACKING
with Small Children

by James H. Stout
and Ann M. Stout

Funk & Wagnalls
New York

 Published simultaneously in Canada by Fitzhenry & Whiteside Limited, Toronto.

Designed by Ingrid Beckman

Manufactured in the United States of America

Library of Congress Cataloging in Publication Data

Stout, James H.
Backpacking with small children.

Bibliography: p.
Includes index.
1. Backpacking. I. Stout, Ann M., joint author. II. Title.
GV199.6.S85 796.5 74-23854
ISBN 0-308-10182-0
1 2 3 4 5 6 7 8 9 10

For Greg and Chris

Contents

Preface

> Yet the universe of the wilderness, all over the United States, is vanishing with appalling rapidity. It is melting away like the last snowbank on some south-facing mountainside during a hot afternoon in June.
>
> —ROBERT MARSHALL, in *Nature*, 1937

If a single motive exists behind the writing of this book, it is the realization that the future preservation of the wilderness areas we so love and cherish is a responsibility that rests with our children. No doubt the initial reaction to this book by many seasoned backpackers will be: "The backcountry is already overtrodden with people—the last thing we need is a lot of kids running around." But truly concerned readers who are aware of the impending dangers to our few remaining sanctuaries must also realize that there exists an urgent need to secure their preservation—not just for next summer or the summer after but for years to come. Bob Marshall's words, above, vividly emphasize in a manner every backpacker can appreciate that the battle for wilderness preservation has been a long one. From the pioneering efforts of John Muir and his followers near the turn of the century to the active conservation groups today, the struggle goes on. And it will certainly be waged for many years to come as efforts continue to preserve our remaining wilderness areas and, hopefully, to add to them. To whom can we entrust these future responsibilities? Certainly not simply to the public, which is largely ignorant of the values at stake.

A few years ago we might have thought first of keeping our favorite backcountry haunts a secret. Today the flooded trailhead parking lots and the number of parties met on the trail is sufficient testimony that there is no secret to keep. We initially cringed at the thought of encouraging families with small children to enter the fragile world of alpine meadows and vistas. Yet this book is written in the belief that our wilderness areas will not endure by trying to keep them secret. The shortsighted solution is to attempt to keep people out; but as our population continues to grow, and more and more people turn to our wildlands, it is clear that just excluding people will not work. Restricting the absolute number allowed in a given area at a given time may be ultimately necessary in all of our national parks and forests, but it is even more important that those who do enter share the responsibility of insuring that the terrain is left unspoiled. One thoughtless camper can do more irreversible damage than a hundred concerned backpackers who are dedicated to keeping the backcountry intact.

It is our hope that by instilling in our children at an early age the proper respect toward nature, we may enable them too to enjoy our greatest heritage. The dedication of this book could hardly be more appropriate, for it is children like our sons Greg and Chris who will eventually bear the burden of the continuing preservation of our wilderness areas.

Backpacking with Small Children

1
Introduction

THE SUN'S RAYS WERE STREAMING through the last remaining conifers at treeline. The jagged crest of the Wind River Range stood protectively to the east; to the west the plains spread out lazily beyond the ridges we had climbed. The expanses of granite and melting snow over which we had traveled that day were now turning to exceptional contrasts of gray and black. As the sun sank in the west, the crest of the Wind River Range just above us began its colorful transformation as the rocks took on a pink and orange alpenglow.

Our two small boys, Gregory, almost five years of age, and Christopher, almost three, played briefly at the stream's sandy edge before coming up the grassy slope to our campsite. Their faces and arms were tanned brown by days above timberline. The smiles on their faces, their laughter, and their willingness to accept the wilderness environment made us feel proud that they could have this opportunity. It had been a long but rewarding day, rich in encounters with nature and with one another. Particularly the day was long for the boys, who had succumbed to every imaginable trailside diversion. Now they were ready for cups of warm soup while the main course of our simple meal was being prepared. Pudding and a bedtime story soon followed, as the alpenglow brightened and then began to darken. Soon the boys were tucked into their down sleeping bags to dream of their many adventures.

We sat together absorbed in the overwhelming solitude about us and the utter simplicity of our lives during the previous days. The many tensions and frustrations of the mechanical outside world had been abandoned fifteen miles behind at the trailhead parking lot. Far more distant was the city and day-to-day existence in a society seemingly bent on self-destruction through material acquisitions. In our vast sanctuary we could not help but think that we were witnessing a delicate remnant of a much grander world that seems to have all but disappeared in the wake of our advancing civilization. All of our country was once like this in the beginning, and now there is so little left: We thought, in that last hour before darkness descended upon us, that if this priceless heritage could have such an impact on our complicated adult lives, what an effect it must have on the rapidly developing characters of our young children. Hopeful that the effect would be a positive one, we too snuggled into our sleeping bags, as the clear sky and crisp air gave promise of another fine day to come.

Only a week earlier, we had been immersed in quite a different life. Like countless other families, for our few weeks' vacation we had wanted to escape from the routine on the home front. We had traveled as far as Cody, Wyoming, when we joined a long westward procession of supercampers, gleaming Airstreams, and assorted three-bedroom mobile homes. Bumpers were ablaze with luminescent stickers attesting to exotic tourist attractions where people had been "getting away from it all."

We were fortunate to find a campsite outside Yellowstone National Park in the early afternoon, having been forewarned that the park's campgrounds were full. We pitched our two small mountain tents amidst the pines, which upon close ex-

The whole point of backpacking with small children is to make it fun and enjoyable for everyone. This is the prerequisite in learning to care for the wilderness.

amination were disfigured with hatchet marks and studded with nails; their scarred trunks had been stripped of branches to the height of a man's reach. The ground cover around our campsite had once been a normal forest floor. Now it consisted of a gray, pulverized mixture of ashes, fliptops, and assorted cigarette butts.

As we attempted to restore the site to an acceptable state, the campground quickly filled with people turned away from sites farther west. Our neighbors on one side were the proud owners of a large camper truck that sprouted a television antenna. Two young boys immediately unloaded a trailbike with which to explore the campground, while their father proceeded noisily to jockey the truck into a level position. In the process, one tall pine took yet another gash in its trunk.

Our neighbors on the other side appeared soon afterward in a huge, lumbering "land yacht." It barely squeezed into the parking area next to ours, making our Volkswagen look like a toy in comparison. The occupants emerged briefly from behind their large, tinted windows to place a bucket beneath their drainpipe before retreating to the obvious comforts of home. Our two small tents pitched in the dust began to look woefully out of place amid the onslaught of other "camping" vehicles. The young trailbikers paused around dinnertime, but the din was soon resumed as they pursued their motorized activity—this time reinforced by a transistor radio which proclaimed once and for all their presence about us.

Fortunately for us and our children, this was only a brief stop on our way to a more rewarding experience. We could not help but wonder, though, what impressions were being formed in the minds of the young trailbikers, and the countless other children of parents whose sole objective is to do Yellowstone in two days, or all of the western states in a week. The child's probable response is boredom, for his interests are usually far removed from those of the adults, whose first concern is often simply covering a certain number of miles. To counteract boredom, every conceivable toy and mechanized diversion are often brought along on the trip so that the kids will be happy. As a result, these children often grow up with no more appreciation or concern for the outdoors than they would have gained in front of the television set back home.

Seeing the indifference of young people toward the real problems facing our vanishing wilderness has provided more than sufficient motivation for the writing of this book. These are the children who will one day assume positions of responsibility and decision in our society. Fortunately, more and more campers are becoming dissatisfied with roadside stopovers, and we are hopeful that more parents among them will share their backpacking experiences with their children.

Several of our backpacking friends have at various times

considered taking their small children on backcountry trips, but then have decided that it would be easier or better to wait until the kids "are a little older," or until they "can appreciate it more." It is *easier* to leave the kids home, for, as will be explained in the following chapters, enjoyable trips with children require a considerable amount of extra planning and mental readjustment. We seriously doubt, however, that it is *better* to leave the kids home. In their preschool years, especially, children are extremely sensitive and responsive to their environment. Much of a child's character and moral fiber is developed in these years, and many of his basic ideas as to how things ought to be done in this world are formed. To deprive your child of sharing your favorite activity in his formative years is to deprive him of an opportunity to develop some of the qualities of a concerned and responsible citizen. The alternative is for one parent to stay home with the kids (or vice versa) while the other goes backpacking. Not only does this destroy a meaningful joint experience for the parents, but the children lose out as well.

The major problem, we have found, which prevents young families from getting on the trail, is a psychological hangup on the part of the parents. Family life without toys, toilets, hot water, and all those modern contrivances which are the foundation of our civilized world seems very problematic indeed. Our ingrown aversion to dirt and nudity, and the anticipation that children won't enjoy primitive living are common deterrents. The problems of finding suitable clothes, equipment, and food and of coping with the limited mobility of small children are important considerations as well. And naturally parents worry about medical care in the event of sickness or accident.

We have attempted to treat each of these problems in various ways in the following chapters. No effort has been made to provide all of the technical knowledge and background necessary for a successful venture into the backcountry with small children. That requires a certain amount of previous backpacking experience on the part of the parents. Without such experience a family outing might well be foolhardy.

Any experienced backpacker can testify to the unpredictable nature of mountain weather, the danger of hypothermia, the effects of snowblindness and overexposure to the sun. With small children along, the seriousness of these hazards is compounded. Several excellent treatises on every aspect of technical backpacking are presently available, but none of these can be considered a substitute for experience on the trail. For this reason we consider this book as a supplement, to be read and used by parents already experienced in back-country travel.

This is a personal narrative, taken from our backpacking and wilderness activities of the past ten or twelve years. We hope that our experiences as related here will show that young children can manage and enjoy a backpacking adventure much more easily than adults often imagine, and that the family group as a whole will benefit by including them.

(In the text, "he" has been used with reference to children instead of "he or she" to facilitate ease of reading. There is no intention to exclude female children.)

2
How Young?

WE HAVE HEARD many discussions of how old a child should be before he is taken backpacking. It is interesting how our friends and acquaintances have answered this question. Some believe that their children should be old enough to appreciate the experience in the same manner as they do. Others feel that the child should be old enough to carry his share of the load (his own sleeping bag, his own clothes, some of the food, etc.). Still other parents maintain that a child should be capable of maintaining an adult pace with adult endurance so that the rest of the group will not be held up. In each case, an average minimum age would seem to be around ten or twelve years old.

When asked, "Why not take the kids backpacking when they are younger?" these parents frequently answer that it is too difficult. But when this activity is deferred to later years, the child's notions of the world have already developed around different activities, usually those of his peers. He has very definite ideas about what things are "cool" or "neat" to do, and even of how they ought to be done. By the time the kids are "old enough" their formative and most impressionable years have passed. Dismayed parents then wonder why their children are not enthusiastic about "roughing it" out in the boonies.

The alternative, exposing a child to wilderness situations at an early age, takes full advantage of those years when many of his basic ideas are formed. The preschool years are probably the most crucial in the child's development of healthy attitudes toward any family activity. Whether it be skiing, canoeing, or backpacking, he is more likely to enjoy it in the company of his parents when he is young than when he is older. We felt it was important for our children to become sensitized to the delicate nature of wilderness before school and neighborhood activities began to dominate their thoughts. Tossing candy wrappers or pop bottles onto a sidewalk is understandable if a child has known nothing else in his upbringing. Cutting down trees for firewood or for building a bridge has no stigma to a young person who has not witnessed those special times when the sun's rays are filtering through a tall stand of fir.

We believe a child should be exposed to wilderness situations at the earliest possible age. This can begin in a preliminary way with infants only a few months old, then extend easily into the toddler stage. After the age of eighteen months or two years, small children can be included successfully in major backpacking activities of a week or two in duration.

Infants and Toddlers

As far as backpacking is concerned, children fall into two well-defined categories: those who are old enough to walk on their own and those who are not. This becomes a very practical distinction when one realizes that by the toddler stage, the child adds an additional twenty-five pounds on someone's back. That weight is equivalent to the total amount of food for two adults and two children on a major backcountry trip. This factor is what limits the total length of a trip. As elaborated in a later chapter, the total weight of nonfood items (tent, sleeping bag, etc.) is essentially constant whether for an overnight or a two-week trip. The only significant remaining variable is food. Thus, if an infant or toddler is to be carried, the length of the trip must be shortened accordingly. We have successfully completed overnight trips with both Greg and Chris when they were infants, but extended trips into the backcountry, which is the real essence of backpacking, were deferred until each boy could walk well.

This by no means excludes less ambitious activities with infants and toddlers. In many ways, small infants are easier to care for than older children. From the time of their birth to three or four months of age, their needs are simple. They must remain warm and dry and be well fed. An infant who is breast-fed is particularly easy to care for, as the need for bottles, formulas, and the like is eliminated.

It is important that an infant of any age enjoy the same sense of security on a backpacking trip as he would enjoy at home. An infant who is two or three months old is less aware of his external environment than when older because he does not actively relate to it. It thus makes little difference to a baby whether he receives his care amid the comforts of home or in a mountain tent, so long as his simple needs are satisfied. This is not to say that an infant notices nothing in an outdoor environment. On the contrary, the flutter of leaves, a gentle breeze, the hum of crickets, the pungency of wildflowers, are all sensations that he undoubtedly enjoys, if not in the same way adults do.

A mother's and a father's attitude toward the infant's experience is all-important, for any apprehension or lack of confidence on the part of the parents could be interpreted by him as an environment less secure than at home. Stress situations involving parents even at home can lead to uneasiness and fussiness on the part of infants.

The infant will have to be protected from standard outdoor

The kiddie pack is a marvelous invention that enables infants and toddlers to join in the fun of backpacking. A hip strap, or "belly band," as on normal backpacks, adds greatly to your stability and comfort. (Photograph courtesy of Suzanne Baizerman)

A sunbonnet and an extra pad are all this young lady needs for an afternoon nap on mom's back. Frequent checks are wise to insure adequate circulation of blood to limbs and that head is in good position. (Photograph courtesy of Michael Baizerman)

hazards—bright sun, mosquitoes, wind, and cold—but with a little thought and preparation ahead of time, these discomforts can be avoided (see Chapter 7).

Backpacking excursions with infants can start as early as two months. There are several carriers made for infants who cannot sit up yet. They omit the frame and support the baby by means of a frontpack made of canvas, cotton, or velveteen. Although we have not had personal experience with this type, friends who have used them rave about how handy they are, at least on day hikes.

The type we have used is for the older infant. At about four months, depending on individual development, an infant develops sufficient strength in his neck and shoulder muscles to be able to sit up. He can then be carried in a device commonly called a "kiddie pack." This marvelous creation comes in several forms, but basically it is a pack frame worn on the back with a bag specially designed to carry an infant. The kind we have used has the child facing forward, an idea we prefer on the adult premise that it is more interesting to see where you are going than where you have already been. More importantly, with this type of kiddie pack, when the infant sleeps he can rest his head on your shoulder. (This positioning becomes a disadvantage in later months, when your hair, eyes, nose, and ears become conveniently reached objects for experimenting small hands.) Since you cannot directly observe what is going on behind your back, you may not be sure what's happened when an uncomfortable position, a mosquito, or the inevitable BM brings discomfort to your young traveler. At moments such as these, it is convenient to have another adult along to survey the situation without your having to unload.

The advantages of a kiddie pack, however, far outweigh the few disadvantages. There is freedom to use both hands, and baby becomes a temporary part of the anatomy, going along on every chore and activity. It is surprising how well infants take to riding in such an apparatus. The natural rhythm of walking, regardless of the terrain, is a terrific pacifier. This undoubtedly stems from familiarity with a mother's everyday rhythm prior to birth. Consequently, an infant may spend most of your walking hours sound asleep on your back, and will commonly awake only when you stop for a breather.

A few improvements can usually be made to make life a bit more enjoyable for your rider. In the earliest months, it is essential that extra padding and support be placed in the front and behind the infant's head. Extra diapers or a small blanket are ideally suited to this purpose. The particular kiddie pack that has served us well through the years has an adjustable cloth seat that can be lowered deep into the body of the pack to give more support to a small baby. It also has a compartment under the seat for supplies. As an added convenience for the carrier, we rigged ours with a belly band to improve walking stability and to distribute weight more equitably. With this arrangement you can safely and comfortably manage more rigorous activities.

Both of our boys when infants enjoyed our cross-country skiing activities on many occasions, and even managed to come along on a downhill skiing venture once. When Greg was thirteen months old, he traveled through most of western Europe in his kiddie pack. All-day excursions in London and Paris, for example, required only Greg's bottle, his blanket, extra diapers, and confidence on our part that we were not subjecting him to hardships.

Confidence in your ability to cope with the normal needs of your child outside the comfortable and familiar home environment increases with experience. There is a natural tendency for parents, particularly those with their first child, to be overprotective and to hesitate to subject young babies to new and different environments. When Greg was old enough to ride in a kiddie pack, we were at first reluctant to venture far away from home or the car for fear something unexpected might suddenly happen to him. It did not take long for us to gain the confidence necessary to cope with normal situations, whether arising in the home or out in the woods. When Chris was born two years later, we didn't hesitate to incorporate him fully and immediately into our outdoor activities.

The time will quickly come when your child takes his first steps, and when there is a glimmer of hope that the kiddie pack can eventually be retired to the attic. The process must be accomplished gradually, however, if the toddler is going to accept easily the transition to self-locomotion. He must be encouraged at every opportunity to walk rather than ride. This would seem simple and natural enough on the surface, but in practice it demands considerable patience on the part of the parents. When you are out on a short day trip, resist the temptation to stick a toddler back into his kiddie pack just because he is not moving along as fast as you would like. Remember, your attitude at this stage may be reflected in his attitude later on. Specifically, if a toddler knows a free ride up the mountain is in store for him when things start to drag a bit on the trail, he may take advantage of this. Small children know as well as anyone else that it is easier and faster to ride than to walk. Moreover, it can be a fine game. You may find that your not-so-exhausted toddler is standing up in his kiddie pack with a stance reminiscent of a Roman chariot—he the Roman and you the chariot!

Small Children

The summer finally arrives when your toddler is sufficiently grown up to walk on his own; he will probably be between the ages of two and a half and four. It all depends on his individual physical development. Your pack is now lightened for an equivalent amount of freeze-dried or other backpacking food. Now the entire family has legs for extended trips into the backcountry. The encouragement you gave your toddler months ago will now hopefully pay off as he attempts to keep up with the fully self-propelled on the trails. His eagerness and enthusiasm at this stage must be nurtured and developed at the same gradual pace as when he took those first steps. His new ability to walk on his own does not mean that long-wished-for forty-mile trip can be suddenly carried off with only the preparation and planning required for an adult venture. Your young backpacker is also at the age when he will evaluate any trip in terms of what he thinks is fun and enjoyable. If the pace set by adults is faster than he wants to manage, he will not enjoy it. If the goals of the trip are exclusively adult goals, like reaching that long-dreamed of golden trout lake before dinner, then you will be disappointed in the performance of your aspiring follower. He will be disappointed too, for a race up the mountain for no reason he can appreciate is not exactly what he had in mind as a fun outing. There are irresistible trailside attractions to entice an inquisitive mind. To expect him to give up

The summer arrives when your child becomes self-propelled on the trail. Lots of encouragement is needed at this stage, like holding hands and keeping the pace slow.

these real and immediate objects that have momentarily captured his interest and fantasy for long-ranged goals that he cannot understand at his age is asking too much.

For this reason, we have long since accepted the fact that the pace and objectives of a backpacking trip must be geared to what is fun and enjoyable for both the kids and the parents. This does not mean that the entire world must revolve around the slightest whim of a child. It does mean, however, that a compromise must be made that is consistent with both your needs and those of your children. Boiled down to its simplest form, it means the entire operation must be *slowed down.* Your attitudes may require some restructuring if you are to retain your sanity and avoid the inevitable frustrations that come when you are not mentally prepared to modify adult ways. This concept is of such importance that it underlies the content of every chapter to follow. Its brief mention here is intended as an introduction to the single

Irresistible trailside attractions will inevitably come up. Forget for a few minutes the adult goals and spend time on the object he is interested in.

most important concept on which many of our ideas have been developed.

The Rewards

Taking extra time and trouble in order to include your children in your camping trips is certainly, in one sense, a bother. Nevertheless we have found the experience invaluable and have given considerable thought to our own motives. There have been exceptional moments, like surveying the entire crest of a mountain range from a serene alpine campsite far above timberline or just simply watching the boys play along a gurgling mountain stream during a break from the trail, when we have felt it was worth the effort a hundred times over. To dissect our feelings any more might take away some of the pure fun and joy of it. One thing is certain: We would not trade one minute of our previous backpacking experiences with the boys for any of the alternative activities available to us. Why? Perhaps we can partially explain by considering some of the broad values we believe to exist and which seem to have contributed most to our enjoyment.

Our own personal motives for backpacking were developed many years ago before our children came upon the scene. We preferred this activity over others because of the natural beauty and solitude only a wilderness area can provide. As we have grown older our personal need for getting far away from the civilized world has increased. The incessant noise, the cars, the relentless competition, the polluted rivers, the masses of humanity—all of this and more seems to bear with increased weight upon our minds and bodies during the course of the winter months. Come spring, we can hardly wait to dig out our gear, check it over, and repair or replace whatever necessary. We begin making mental plans for a major outing months in advance. Just the anticipation is enough to preserve our sanity until the departure date. For us, a two-week stint at a fashionable resort or an auto trip across the country and back will not accomplish the rehabilitation that is needed. We have to really get away from it all, with nothing about us for as far as we can see but high mountains and precious solitude. This is a personal need we satisfied by backpacking before our children came along, and it remains a basic need even as parents.

In some cases, it is entirely possible to leave small children with relatives or close friends for a few days or even a week at a time. For us, this period of time is barely adequate to really get into it. True, you can physically cover a lot of ground in a week's time, but it usually takes us a couple of days on the trail before we can mentally shake off the trials and pressures that remain back home. Having a willing babysitter for more than a week is an exceptional situation, however, and usually other alternatives must be entertained. One is for one of the parents to stay home with the kids while the other goes cavorting over the hills. We have excluded this alternative, not because each of us does not enjoy the outdoors in our own way but because our enjoyment is enhanced when together. If both parents really want and need to get out, but one must remain at home with the kids, you can be assured that a marriage will not be any better for it.

In short, one of the more important reasons for incorporating your small children into backpacking activities is so you yourself can continue to enjoy the outdoors. You may find, as we have, that your children will grow up loving the things you do simply because those are the things you enjoy doing most and you have made it possible for them to do it with you.

Perhaps even a better reason for backpacking with children at a very young age is the exceptional family experience it can provide. We have felt a more meaningful and closer relationship between ourselves and our children when we are isolated from the office, the freeways, and the mass media. The total lack of civilized diversions that only adults indulge in, like the afternoon cocktail or the weekly card game, places everyone in the family on an equal footing. Suddenly you have an incredible number of things in common with your child. You might be surprised in such a situation how immersed you can become in the activities of your children—particularly on a sunny day in certain alpine meadows with their infinite variety of flowers, rocks, and insects. You will be utterly amazed at the wonders a small child can see and appreciate that seem to pass us adults by. There is such a beautiful simplicity to the life of a small child. The things he sees, feels, and appreciates seem at first insignificant from the viewpoint of our infinitely complicated lives. But once the concerns back home are cast away a fresh and sometimes new dimension appears to make the trip even more rewarding.

One of the most important factors that will dictate the success (or failure) of such a backpacking trip is the overall objective that is set. If dad sets goals that interest only him and mom is along just to care for the kids, and the children are along just to behave themselves and not get in the way, then there will be problems. Momentary periods of frustration or anxiety are likely to become total roadblocks. The result may be so discouraging that next time mom and the kids will *prefer* to stay home while dad goes fishing or mountain climbing.

A far healthier attitude for all concerned is to consider the trip a family affair at the outset. This is not to say dad should give up that irresistible trout pool—just that it should not be the guiding light around which everything must revolve and around which everything may eventually tumble down. There is no reason objectives cannot be decided upon beforehand that are consistent with everyone's desires. So you don't make that fabled lake by nightfall. Big deal. You will probably make it by noon on the next day and have the entire afternoon to enjoy it.

You've probably heard friends say, "Boy, I wish I could get away from the job and spend some time with the family."

Dad is away from the house every day except weekends as a general rule and sometimes he's not home even then. When Saturday comes, the lawn needs mowing, the fence is in need of repair, or a weekend hobby needs attending. Sunday arrives with church, perhaps a game of golf, more chores around the house, and if all goes well, there may be time for a short drive out of town and back with the family. Suddenly Monday morning appears, and it all starts over again. Week after week, month after month, and before long everyone is screaming to get out of the rut. Spring finally comes with the prospect of a two-week vacation in the not too distant future. Take the opportunity then to start planning a backpacking trip with the whole family. Everyone will love it!

This chapter would be incomplete if some mention were not made of the possible effects of wilderness experiences on children in their preschool years. If child psychologists are agreed on one thing, it is that their understanding of the mechanisms of early behavioral development is far from complete. One thing does seem certain—the early learning experience must be rich and varied in order that a child may intelligently cope with the ever-changing and complex world. It must be kept in mind that a child's comprehension of the world comes by interacting with it in a very direct way. In the case of a wilderness experience, this may mean scrambling up a giant slab of granite with square miles of the same in every direction or gazing up the trunk of a 150-foot pine with thousands of others like it in the background. Feeling the bark, sticking small fingers into worm holes, or experiencing the sharpness of its needles are all meaningful to a child. These are things that cannot be transmitted to a small child verbally either at home or in the classroom. He must discover them through active learning on the spot.

Your child may even be at the age when learning processes such as these cannot as yet be expressed on the verbal level. They may not even be internalized as concrete mental notions. Yet impressions are being made, and with them your child is acquiring some of the many basic building blocks that he uses to integrate and interpret new experiences. All you must do as a parent is to provide him the opportunity to learn and to have faith in his capacity to learn.

Many parents tend to underestimate the impact of their own presence and behavior on their young children. Entire patterns of behavior like the development of self-reliance and independence, and hopefully an appreciation of nature, can be formed in the preschool years. At this stage, the parent provides essentially the only model for behavior. As the child grows older, influences outside of the family become gradually more important. At age five or six, formal schooling becomes the dominant environmental factor, and much of your child's future development is then in someone else's hands.

It is for this reason that the preschool years are so important. In the absence of other peer-group influences, they are probably the most formative and impressionable years of your child's life. His introduction to backpacking during these years is likely to be more successful in terms of the freedom and fullness of his reactions than in later years. His developing attitudes at this stage are extremely important, for the impressions he forms will likely provide the basis for additional experiences later on in his life. Healthy parental attitudes toward the preservation of natural things will likely breed similar attitudes in children, and if that is accomplished, a long step will have been taken toward the wilderness education of our young people.

3

Planning and Preparation

THERE ARE MANY REWARDS that come from a carefully planned backpacking trip. The preparations must begin long before you actually heft your pack and get on the trail. The purpose of this chapter is to highlight some of the extra preparations which would normally not be considered on an "adult-only" trip. Answers to a few of the more obvious questions like "where to go?" or "for how long?" depend on several factors, all of which should be evaluated according to the capabilities of your family. Specific equipment needs and sometimes the specific route you decide upon require special attention as well.

In addition to the physical aspects of preparations, there is a certain attitude that must be developed. This includes acceptance of the fact that the pace and objectives of the trip will be pared down to what the kids can manage. If you plan ahead, you won't be impatiently twiddling your thumbs while the kids are engaged in some trailside attraction. We have fond memories of reading a favorite paperback novel in the warm sun near a stream where the boys were busily constructing sand castles.

The extent to which extra preparations will be required depends on how outdoor-oriented your family is to begin with. Walking has always been a way of life for us. We simply enjoy walking to a destination instead of driving. Our enthusiasm was enhanced by Greg and Chris's eagerness to walk at an early age. Neither boy was particularly fond of his strol-

Time out to enjoy the discoveries small children can make in an alpine meadow. These are simple things like flowers, rocks, and insects, but are all meaningful to a child.

ler or even his kiddie pack. On an afternoon's outing to the grocery store three blocks away, for example, Greg at thirteen months of age preferred to push his stroller most of the way there and back. Children need and enjoy exercise just as adults. We don't expect our children to sit down to a meal with healthy appetites or to even sleep well if they have been cooped up inside all day. That is perhaps why our children have taken so naturally to backpacking. They really prefer an active, outdoor life, and backpacking is one way to fulfill this need.

Another prerequisite that becomes important in the planning stages is that the whole family enjoys and is accustomed to car-camping. Asking a mother of small children to don a pack with a week's provisions for the wilderness when she has never even pitched a tent is ridiculous. It is not that she could not do it! It is rather that she would not feel comfortable without some previous outdoor living experience. You have to organize *yourself* for this change before you can plan for small children's needs. Backpacking takes off where car-camping stops, and car-camping itself is quite different from one's household. The cookware is different, and so is the stove. The beds are different as is the roof! It is easiest to make the transition from house to car-camping and then to backpacking. An ideal approach is to car-camp when the child is too small to walk comfortably by himself and when more paraphernalia is considered necessary (at least by most parents) for his comfort. By the time the child can enjoy longer periods of hiking, he will already be used to sleeping bags, tents, cook kits, and the whole outdoor situation. Then the prospect of toting the equipment on one's back becomes the only new variable. Introducing too many variables at once can be upsetting to any child.

Sharing the Preparations

Children love to be included in adult affairs and will enjoy the feeling that they are really helping to plan a family excursion. A two-year-old could be asked if he likes the freeze-dried applesauce you are planning to serve him for the next five days, or if he thinks his new sleeping bag will be comfortable enough. Regardless of his answers, he immediately becomes involved, and his interest and curiosity will mount. A three- or four-year-old will enjoy looking at catalogs filled with pictures of equipment. Questions like "Which tent looks like the most fun to sleep in?" or "Do you think the tent will be big enough for all of us?" will do much to generate enthusiasm. With this background, a trip to a local sporting goods store with tents set up on display can be a real adventure. It is amazing how much small children understand. Their greatest fear is that they won't get to go. Reassure them early that they are important members of the expedition.

Talk about the trip should be enough to arouse interest and a sense of togetherness but not so much as to get the child overly excited. Anyone with young children knows it is a mistake to say, "We are going to Grandma's house next week." For six days you will be asked "We going to Granma's now?" Instead more general conversation, such as "What kind of cookies did you have at Grandma's the last time we were there?" will guarantee the child's interest in Grandma. The small child has no conception of next week or next month and will only be disappointed that he isn't going immediately if a trip is discussed in a time context. Three days before the departure date of a major trip one summer our four-and-a-half-year-old was unusually quiet all morning. He had hardly said a word all during breakfast. We knew he had something on his mind and was giving it considerable thought. Finally it came out: "Dad, are we leaving day after tomorrow?" The departure day seemed an eternity away.

Also, both children were very anxious to speed up the preparations so we could leave sooner. They really wanted to help but of course seemed to be underfoot most of the time. It takes extra patience on the part of parents to think of constructive ways to let the children help during those last days. Sometimes the completion of a simple task by an adult becomes a major project with two small boys. But we feel that it is better to let the boys help when they are willing and actually volunteering, and then to redo the task if necessary, than to ignore them or turn them away because they are too little. Much of the fun and anticipation of a big trip is in the planning and preparation, and we should not deprive the kids of this. Our boys had great fun ripping off extra cardboard packaging for our food bags, fetching marking pens, and actually helping label our meal bags. The important thing to remember is that the kids will enjoy backpacking if they have had a part in preparing for it.

Where to Go?

Before you can proceed with specific preparations you have to decide on the general location and nature of your trip. Will it be in a mountainous area, a desert area, a rainy coastal location? The locality with its terrain and weather will determine the type of equipment, food, and clothing you will need.

Much can be said in favor of high mountainous regions, especially when very small children are involved. Because they are small, kids are particularly vulnerable to poisonous snakes, spiders, and plants. It is exceedingly difficult to impress upon a small child the consequences of a snake or scorpion bite. It is best to avoid such environments until your kids are older and can better look out for such hazards. This can be done by restricting your backpacking activities to elevations above 5,000 feet where these dangers are less likely to be found.

Also, the time of year you choose for your trip will affect the specific routes you may be considering. In high mountains, particularly in the western part of the country, the snowpack can persist well into July. This makes for slippery and slow going when children are along. Streams and rivers are likely to be higher and more difficult to cross in the springtime as well. It is one thing for an adult to make a stream crossing, but with a child in tow it becomes quite another matter.

The climate of the region may also influence your route. In mountainous regions with high summer rainfall or frequent thunderstorms with accompanying lightning, you may prefer to remain below timberline. In areas like the Sierras, this presents less of a problem because of the infrequent regional storms.

If you do decide upon a mountainous region, most of the country's national forests and parks will provide good possibilities. Although many of our national parks are overcrowded, it is impressive how the population thins just a mile or so from the road. Even in our most popular recreational areas, like Yosemite and Yellowstone, only a small proportion of tourists will venture beyond sight of their cars or camper trucks.

Most nationally supervised areas will have a well-established network of backcountry trails. This becomes important not only for navigational purposes but it expedites moving your family away most efficiently from civilization.

Once you have narrowed your choice to a couple of places, or even to a specific area, investigate the availability of maps. Most major cities in the country have map shops or bookstores that carry trail maps and topographic maps of the most popular national forests and parks. In the event they have no maps of your area in stock, they usually have U.S. Geological Survey index maps showing what maps are available. Such shops will normally order these maps for you, or you can write for them yourself. For topographic maps write to the U.S. Geological Survey, Map Distribution Section, Federal Bldg., Denver, Colorado 80225. These indices are free of charge and will show what topographic maps are available at what scale and price. Take particular note of the date of an index, because topographic coverage of many unmapped areas is currently being prepared, and these will not be included in an outdated index. In some cases, prepublication copies of new maps are available but may contain small errors in printing, etc. When ordering your maps, it is often helpful to get the shaded, woodland version. This costs no more, and especially in places above timberline, the woodland shading is helpful in planning routes and campsites.

The U.S. Forest Service has excellent trail maps of national forests and wilderness areas. Write for area maps to the U.S. Forest Service, Dept. of Agriculture, Washington, D.C., 20225. Most national parks have wilderness areas under their jurisdiction. For their publications write to the National Park Service, Dept. of the Interior, Washington, D.C., 20225.

However, the forest service maps we have seen and used include wilderness boundaries, access roads, natural surface features, but *no* topographic lines. Thus the nature of the terrain must be inferred from the drainage pattern which is usually, but not always, shown. These maps, however, reveal little of the actual relief, hindering you from reliably determining beforehand between a gentle climb and a steep one. Thus, we recall taking an eleven-day trip with the boys in August 1972 from Elkhart Park on the west flank of the Wind River Range to Elbow Lake just five miles southwest of Gannett Peak, the highest point in Wyoming. The climb via Island Lake and Jean Lakes was relatively easy, amounting to about a 1,500-foot increase in elevation. An alternative route was taken by a group of four adults whom we met near Elbow Lake. It involved hiking downhill to Fremont Creek, 2,000 feet *below* where they had begun the hike. That was the easy part. Then came the long steep climb to regain the lost elevation plus the additional climb to Summit Lake and finally to Elbow. A quick glance at a topographic map would have revealed the awkwardness of their route. Had children been among the victims of this lack of planning, it would have been a long haul indeed.

It is wiser from the point of view of both children and adults to patronize the less challenging grades. It is surprising, though, how a child will respond to a series of steep switchbacks whereas an hour earlier a long gentle slope had become tiresome.

Even topographic maps may not show water sources accurately. As safe water is a primary concern with freeze-dried foods, it is wise when in doubt to write to the appropriate forest service office, in advance, asking whether the water is drinkable from the lakes and streams you plan to encounter on your trip. Many changes can come to a lake or stream over the years, such as eutrification or chemical changes in the water quality due to fires. We once planned a week-long trip out of Big Sandy in the southern Wind River Range but decided against it at the last minute upon learning from the local ranger that sheep were allowed to graze in that area during August. This fact was known in the area, and people didn't hike there because they knew it had been a grazing place for sheep.

Remember, carrying other than a minimal volume of water is out of the question in most mountainous areas, so you would be wise to choose your route around available water sources. Besides, kids just adore running water!

When you write for maps, you can also inquire about the conditions of the trails you plan to use. The forest service or park rangers have usually hiked or ridden horseback over the major trails in the area and will know of any trails that are closed or those that may have just opened. On one trip we encountered a new trail not shown on our map. It was headed in the direction we were going, so we tried it and saved ourselves about two miles and about 500 feet of elevation. In general it is best to stick to known trails, but in this case we had been hiking in the area for about three weeks and felt well oriented. We also guided ourselves carefully with the topographic map. If you have to choose between a topographic map and a forest service map, choose the former. Ideally, get both.

If you decide to order maps on your own, be sure to do it well ahead of time. Maps ordered from the U.S. Geological Survey in February may be obtained in about two weeks' time, but the same maps ordered in May can take more like six weeks! Similarly, order your U.S. Forest Service maps from divisional offices before they are caught up in the inevitable spring rush. For an extra thirty-five cents you can get your maps by airmail in four to five days.

For How Long?

The duration of your trip will depend on two factors. First, it depends on how much previous experience you have had. It is foolhardy to attempt a week-long trip if your family has never been on an overnight one. Perhaps the best approach is to start off with an overnight or weekend trip and then go on to longer trips after you have gained the confidence and experience to do so.

Secondly, the maximum length of a trip in most cases is dictated by the load you are willing to carry at the outset. The basic pack excluding food remains essentially constant whether it be for an overnight or for a ten-day trip. Our experience has been that seven to eight days of food for two adults and two children is about the maximum we feel comfortable with in addition to the basic packload. Of course, you can extend your stay in the backcountry by supplementing your diet with fresh fish and berries. This will be discussed later.

Planning Your Equipment Needs

If this is to be your first backpacking trip with small children, it will require some time to procure the necessary equipment. The many considerations here are of such importance that a later chapter is devoted entirely to them. In the planning stages of your trip, however, you should survey the available child-sized items in local retail stores and in mail-order catalogs. It will take a week to a month to obtain through the mail catalogs listed in Chapter 4.

Perhaps there are items you can borrow from backpacking friends, or you might decide, as we did, to make some of your own equipment. Four years ago, we could not find quality down sleeping bags and parkas in small enough sizes, and larger sizes were not suitable. Our only alternative was to plan and construct these items to our own specifications (see Chapter 4). If you choose this alternative, you will have to shop around for materials such as zippers of the proper length, fabric, etc. This will take some time, so don't put it off. If you decide on one of several commercial kits (see Chapters 4 and 6), allow several weeks' shipping time and then additional time necessary for assembly.

Visits to mountaineering stores can be helpful in planning your equipment needs and at the same time provide outings for the whole family. These stores specialize in backpacking and are good places to get specific ideas about what type of tent, sleeping bags, and cooking equipment will best suit your family. These places also provide a good introduction to your child of what backpacking is all about. Our kids couldn't wait to get into that display tent, for example. And why not? They are meant to be scrutinized. Check with the clerk to be sure there's no problem with your children's explorations, but within reason, there shouldn't be. The ease with which your youngest gets in and out of a mountain tent may well be a deciding factor in a tent purchase!

Kids should be encouraged to share in the planning and preparation. The prospect of purchasing a new tent is exciting business. Let them participate.

Sometimes mail-order firms have a better selection or more reasonable prices than your local retail stores (see Chapter 4). Some catalogs offer off-season sales on popular tents and sleeping bags.

Planning Your Menus

Wintertime is not too soon to start experimenting with freeze-dried and instant foods. The possibilities are so numerous as to be absolutely mindboggling. The choice ranges from complete freeze-dried meals to what your own imagination dictates in the compilation of homemade casserole and bread mixes. (See Chapter 5 for recipes.) It seems that the supermarkets have new instant products on the shelves every week. If you don't mind preservatives you might want to pick up one to try each week just for fun. Taste, subjective and demanding as it is, is not something to leave to trial and error on the trail. You don't want to be cooking food no one likes, or that isn't filling, or that takes twice as long to prepare as you thought it would. All these possible problems can be worked out ahead of time. This way you assure minimum hassles on the trail and maximum comfort for everyone.

Getting Down to Essentials

With the gathering of equipment, it becomes important to keep in mind those items which are essential and those which are not. This means that as the planning progresses you must continually ask: "Do I really need this or that?," or perhaps more directly, "Do I really want to carry this or that?" Every extra item adds extra weight. And when you are carrying for children it is ever so important to pare off those extra ounces. This means employing all of the weight-saving techniques you know and then some. There are several excellent books available that deal at length with how to cut down the weight on one's back. But in the final analysis, we have found it far better to do without a nonessential item than go to great extremes to obtain an ultralight version of the same. A good example is a lightweight lantern or even a candle lantern. It is convenient to have such an item at night for reading, but it is not essential. We prefer to go to sleep with the children when it gets dark, and as a result, we get up earlier to do our reading.

Sometimes it is difficult at first to decide what is essential and what is not. A wise choice comes only with experience. Through the years, we have made mental notes of those items that were never used or rarely used on our backpacking trips. For example, at one time we carried knife-fork-spoon

Here are some of our essentials and nonessentials all laid out before organizing into packs. We consider our stove and extra fuel in the "essential" category for ecological and safety reasons.

combinations in neat little kits on all of our trips. We discovered after a while that we never used the knives, and we rarely used the forks. The spoons, however, were always used and thus became essential items. Our children, in fact, prefer to use spoons for all kinds of eating rather than forks.

Another example is plates. These rather inefficiently shaped receptacles can be totally done away with. A slightly flared bowl is a better choice, but a large cup can serve all of your eating purposes quite adequately. If you have a large item to eat, like a trout for instance, it is more efficient to cut it up so it fits your cup rather than to bring along extra dishes of the proper size. We routinely bone all fish in the pan they were cooked in, then serve the boned pieces in cups or bowls depending on how many dishes we feel like washing.

By making observations like these, your list of "essentials" becomes smaller and smaller. For two adults and two children our list runs something like this:

1 mountain tent with fly
4 sleeping bags, 2 stuff sacks
4 pads
1 cook kit containing 3 nesting aluminum pots (1-, 2- and 3-quart)
4 large plastic cups
4 medium plastic bowls
4 spoons
1 pocketknife
matches (about 40 in 2 waterproof match cases)
1 plastic mesh dishwashing scourer
1 small sponge
1 4-ounce plastic dispenser bottle of liquid biodegradable soap (Shakley's Basic H is excellent)
1 Teflon-coated aluminum 9-inch frypan for pancakes, fish, etc.
1 aluminum quart container filled with white gas
1 small dish towel
1 small face towel
1 wash cloth
1 aluminum trowel
1 one-burner mountain stove (ours is a Svea)
1 change of clothes for everyone
1 set extra wool socks for everyone
down parkas for everyone
rain gear or ponchos for everyone
1 small soap bar (hotel size)
1 small toothpaste and 4 toothbrushes
½ roll toilet paper
quart poly bottle for water or other liquids
maps
compass
first-aid kit

1 Mallory flashlight
insect repellent, suntan lotion
two or three paperbacks (for kids and adults)
packs and frames

This is a remarkably small list, but it represents, in our opinion, the equipment items one *must* have to undertake a safe and enjoyable trip. These items form the nucleus of every trip we take, whether it be a simple overnight or a two-week venture. Some backcountry devotees will argue that a tent is not essential, and certainly there are many situations where it seems unnecessary. But for reasons given in the following chapter, we would not take our children into isolated areas without one.

Inclusion of additional items to the essential list will vary from family to family. For example, we nearly always include our Svea 123 stove with an additional quart of fuel. Sure, this is nonessential from the point of view that we could manage without it. But we believe in preserving the natural deadfall whenever possible, particularly in the high alpine regions where we most frequently travel. So we add two pounds of fuel to our essential list for an overnight trip and three pounds for extended trips where extra fuel is needed.

Our essential items amount to around fifty pounds. This is divided between two adults. The only remaining variable is food, and that will depend on the duration of your trip. On short trips, you have the opportunity to enjoy a relatively light pack, providing you avoid the temptation to throw on the kitchen sink just because you are not loaded to full capacity. In such situations, we usually decide to include the niceties of everyday life to some extent. The preparations around our house for a trip are never complete without a discussion on the pros and cons of a spatula. Even though you can manage to turn a trout or even a pancake with a spoon, we generally end up toting a plastic spatula along. Each family will prefer different luxuries. We once ran into a middle-aged woman and her two teen-age daughters on a backcountry trail in Wyoming. They had finished a thirty-mile loop and were heading out when we exchanged the usual hellos. As the woman passed by, we stared in amazement at the roll of paper towels attached with a special clamp to the back of her pack.

It is important to include on your list of essentials your child's particular security item(s). The child's needs will depend on his age. Up until Christopher was over three years old, he needed diapers and a bottle of milk before he could go to bed. During that period one eight-ounce plastic bottle proved adequate on all of our backpacking trips. We always rinsed it out with clean water right after use and found we did not need to bring a bottle brush. With a bottle, of course, extra milk must be packed. Dried milk comes in a variety of fat contents all conveniently prepackaged in quart envelopes. Vigorous shaking of the dry milk in cold water will make a palatable drink. The children have never complained about it except when an occasional undissolved lump gets stuck inside a bottle nipple. Here it pays to try out different brands at home first and see which ones shake up best.

If your child is really dependent on his security item, a backpacking trip is not the time to wean him from it. If he needs a pacifier to get to sleep take two of them. You want him to feel comfortable in this new activity. We know a child who routinely used to lose his "pacer," causing no end of problems until his parents got the idea of tying it to his clothing. No more lost and dirty pacifiers. If your child needs his favorite blanket to get to sleep, it may be necessary to carry it along. Perhaps he can carry it in his own little pack. Some parents have successfully gotten away with carrying a piece of the blanket. We never could.

If you are unsure whether your child can get along without his favorite thing, whatever it is, there are two choices. You can try to get him over it several months ahead of time so that he is not likely to notice its absence on your trip, or you can just plan on carrying it. This is obviously the safer plan as a new situation may make his need for that animal or bottle

Security items are a must if the well-being of your child depends on it. There were times when Chris had to have his bottle, even on the trail.

stronger. If by some chance your two-year-old is hooked on a four-pound metal fire truck, better figure out a lightweight plastic substitute!

Kids can be pretty determined about what they think is important. We had a pretrip discussion with Greg when he was four and a half years old about how much easier it would be if we didn't have to carry his blanket. Greg agreed it was too heavy and took up too much room in the pack. Besides, we felt Greg was really too old to be dragging his ratty old blanket around. Score one, or so we thought. When we arrived at our campsite on our first night out, there was Greg's blanket. It mysteriously appeared from the depths of his down bag—a genuine stowaway!

The Backyard Pretrip

Once you have assembled your basic equipment, it is important that the entire family become familiar with it before plunging out into the wilds. Small children easily forget the camping experiences of previous summers, so a backyard camping trip is frequently in order just to insure that everyone is at ease with the idea. There the tent can be set up in a familiar environment where the kids can fully explore it. Let them unroll and arrange their sleeping bags in the tent, giving *them* the opportunity to choose exactly where they want to sleep. Then encourage them to arrange the adult bags as well so there is room for everyone. Develop the attitude that a small tent full of billowy down sleeping bags is a fun place to sleep rather than an undesirable confinement.

Around the age of three or four years, children begin fantasy play and have incredible imaginings. Frequently the line between the real world and the imaginary one becomes very fine. The last thing you want is for your small backpacker to imagine that those tree shadows are monsters coming at him through the tent walls. Tents are lots of fun for kids, and they usually have no difficulty adjusting to them as long as they have had some prior familiarity with them.

The backyard trip is also the time to make note of any repairs that are needed. Don't wait to discover that torn mosquito netting until you're five miles from the nearest road. Sticky zippers are a nuisance, too, especially when you, the kids, *and* the mosquitoes are simultaneously trying to get into the tent. A bit of silicon spray or other metal lubricant solves that problem.

It is also a good idea at this time to check your tent and fly for leaks. The backyard hose provides a fair simulation of an afternoon thundershower and will reveal any leaks. Let your children help spot those leaks by having them in the tent while you apply the "rain." Take particular note of leaky seams, especially between the tent fabric and the splash guard.

Adjustment to a sleeping bag should not present a problem if you plan ahead. Realize first that a child spends approximately one-half of his life in a crib or bed perched a couple of feet off the floor. To suddenly spend those hours in a sleeping bag at ground level represents quite a change.

Greg and Chris adjusted rather easily to their sleeping bags. This was due, in part, to our insistence that their bags be of comparable quality and comfort to our own. Because they observed and participated in the construction of their bags at home, there was nothing strange about them. Being able to see and feel the raw materials increased their familiarity with their bags, though in this case at the cost of having part of a two-pound bag of prime goose down spread around our bedroom. It was simply irresistible to our inquisitive three-year-old.

Although the boys were quite excited at the prospect of trying out their very own sleeping bags, we anticipated possible objections to sleeping on the floor. So one week before we were to go car-camping with the new bags, we introduced them in place of the boys' regular blankets on their beds. After a couple of nights of that, they were ready to try sleeping on the floor with their pads "just like camping." In retrospect, perhaps this procedure was unnecessary. However, the boys were never at all reluctant to use their bags, so perhaps the precaution was worthwhile. Chris is so secure with his bag that one morning last winter we discovered him snuggled inside of it beneath his regular bed!

Day Trips

An important part of preparations is breaking in new boots and packs. Day trips in the spring are a good time for this. We bought new boots (see Chapter 6) for the boys in April so there would be ample time for breaking them in prior to the summer. The boys experimented with their small day packs (see Chapter 4) as well, so the time spent in our local parks served a double purpose.

A good reason for day trips prior to a big trip is to get everyone in the family out walking. You are probably planning to cover a mile or two on the first day of your backpacking trip. What if your children have never walked that far? They will not miraculously sprout wings and fly up the trail. If you routinely carry your child after walking just a block at home, he will expect to be carried after a short distance on a trail. The idea is to demonstrate to your child through your own example that walking is fun. You can walk to interesting places and see interesting things on the way. By doing this as a family, children will accept walking as a normal mode of transportation and look forward to it. In short, day trips covering a mile or two become a happy family time together.

After you have exhausted your local parks, you can take on more ambitious objectives. A good example was a trip we made into Devil's Canyon in Angeles National Forest. Out of sheer desperation to escape the Los Angeles smog one fall morning, we hurriedly packed a lunch, day packs, the boys, and ourselves into our Volkswagen, and within ninety minutes we were overlooking the whole area from the Angeles Crest Highway. Starting from the top and hiking down the canyon was an easy way to start out. Greg, age three at the time, had a fantastic time leading the way down the trail. Chris, age fifteen months, toddled on down with only an occasional helping hand. Three and a half miles later, and at the bottom, we had lunch and enjoyed a refreshing wade in the cool water of the creek. After exploring the stream and its variety of rocks, logs, and sandbars, we were ready to head back up. By that time, Chris was ready for his nap, so into the kiddie pack he went. There he remained, sound asleep, for the remainder of the afternoon. Greg managed the climb up entirely on his own. The idle time spent relaxing at the bottom had paid off.

Longer day trips such as this give you a good idea of what to expect from your kids and from yourself as well. The Devil's Canyon trip was most encouraging, for we were planning on at least a couple of backpacking trips in the Sierras the following summer (see Chapter 9). With the entire winter and spring ahead of us to get physically and mentally into shape, we knew at that time we would encounter no major difficulties hiking with small children.

4

Equipment—Quality For All

NOW THAT YOU ARE CONVINCED, hopefully, that backpacking with small children *is* feasible, what special or extra equipment needs will you have? We have found from experience that quality child-sized equipment is an essential ingredient for a successful backpacking trip. Some backpacking parents may contend that the kids can manage with hand-me-down adult sleeping bags, tennis shoes, and other items from around the house. This is true to some extent, but there are two very good reasons why you and your children will benefit in the long run by using better quality items.

First, you are expecting your children to participate in an outdoor activity on an equal basis with you, except that the pace of the whole operation will be scaled down to their abilities. Good-quality boots are as essential to their physical well-being as to yours. You are also expecting them to sleep under the same sky as adults. You can be certain that a small child will enjoy the warmth and comfort of a down sleeping bag every bit as much as you enjoy yours. The down shirt you so enjoy when the sun drops below the distant peaks will feel equally comforting to him as well. Experienced backcountry travelers will appreciate the virtues of quality equipment. It follows that no unnecessary compromise of that standard should be made for the rest of the family.

Second, there is real psychological value to equipping your children in the same manner as you would equip yourself. Right from the planning stages of your trip, their ideas and opinions should be sought if only for the purpose of enhancing their interest and enthusiasm. They will quickly realize that this is no ordinary vacation, but one that involves doing things that are normally geared only for adults. Children frequently will not really become enthused about an activity unless they think they have the proper things to do it with. For example, we started Greg at age five on cross-country skis, using an old pair of skis cut down to reasonable dimensions and mounted with cable bindings fit to his existing boots. He had watched us and others on numerous occasions and was eager to give it a try. But for some reason, he did not respond with the enthusiasm we had anticipated. Later, the reason came out. His skis did not have the sleek, lightweight pin bindings that ours had. That was soon remedied. He found it was much easier to learn the balance with the lighter bindings and now really enjoys the sport.

This principle applies to backpacking equipment as well. This means wearing boots like mom and dad, carrying a pack like mom and dad, and having one's very own sleeping bag. This may seem a bit excessive at first, but when a healthy attitude toward the activity is at stake, these extra considerations will prove worthwhile.

After scrounging through your existing gear, a trip to your local sporting goods store or mountain shop will probably be in order. This will quickly reveal two things. First, you may find little in the way of equipment tailored to small backpackers. Second, when the salesman becomes convinced that you are serious about this matter, he will either conclude that you are in need of immediate psychiatric care or he will suggest you talk to the mobile home dealer across the street.

A trip to your local library or bookstore may prove equally

Plain, old-fashioned walking is a marvelous way to travel. It can get you to some of the nicest places.

discouraging. There are volumes written on the fine points of backpacking, and these cover everything from clipping labels off tea bags to save weight to cleaning the fuel line on a Primus stove. Some chapters will be devoted to the most minute details of high-quality sleeping bags, tents, boots, and the like, but these will cater almost exclusively to adult requirements. So you look further down the shelf for books on family camping. A few minutes perusing reveals that camping of any sort with small children means mostly camping by car, trailer, or some other motorized vacation vehicle.

Why? Part of the reason is that our culture is vehicle-oriented. You can find articles on how to manage children in motorboats, on trailbikes, and even in snowmobiles. But try and find something on walking with your child in the woods. Walking is slow, inefficient, and may even involve some old-fashioned perspiration. Fortunately, the ranks of people who really dig this outdated mode of transportation are growing. Manufacturers have long been aware of the need for proper adult equipment. Finally, we are starting to see some items specifically tailored for small children. Just recently several nationally known department stores started to carry hiking boots with Vibram soles in children's sizes. Now all the kids in our neighborhood are wearing them. A local sporting goods store near us recently stocked twelve child-sized pack frames, and they were sold out in three days. Even good quality children's sleeping bags and parkas are beginning to appear.

In the following sections, we give special consideration to those equipment items that require special tailoring when small children are involved. We have made no attempt whatsoever to provide a comprehensive treatment of all of the equipment necessary for a normal adult trip. There are other good texts which discuss these aspects.

Tents

Several authorities on adult backpacking emphasize that in many situations considerable weight can be spared by foregoing the luxury of a tent. In the event of an afternoon shower, a poncho or a welcoming fir tree will provide reasonable protection. In case of a regional downpour, most adults can slosh back to the civilized world even when wet to the bone. Most experienced backpackers can recall such situations. We recall a memorable trip in the Sierras several years ago when a major Pacific storm caught us unprepared. We departed under clear skies in early July near Mammoth Mountain on the east side of the range. On the return trip eight lovely days later, we spent our last night above Shadow Lake just east of the Minarets. We saved considerable weight by not bringing a tent, and in view of the fine weather we had experienced, it seemed justified. Around 4:00 P.M., an ominous bank of clouds loomed to the west, and the wind picked up. Later in the evening, as we crawled into our sleeping bags, the sky was completely clouded over. As a token precaution, we placed a small coated ground cloth over our bags in case it did rain. It did. Around 1:00 A.M. it began to sleet. By 3:00 A.M. an inch of very soggy snow covered everything. Our hastily improvised shelter worked for a while, but our highly absorbent down sleeping bags performed like sponges in the highly humid atmosphere. It seemed as if morning would never come. When it did, the precipitation had turned to a saturating rain. We finally slogged out in the mess, arriving at our car early in the afternoon. Although we had put ourselves in a potentially very dangerous situation, our physical activity in the process of hiking out in the near freezing rain provided all of the body heat we needed. Our bags were completely soaked through. We were too, as much from body perspiration as from the incessant rain.

Had we been another day's journey from our destination, an additional night out could have spelled disaster. Our bags could not have possibly dried out. Fortunately, we learned this lesson in our prefamily years, with no children to contend with.

Since we have been backpacking with our children, we have come to appreciate two hazards of foul weather. First, the mind of a small child does not grasp the potential consequences of getting completely wet. There is no way known to man to keep a child dry in pouring rain when he is walking on his own. Second, when he *does* get wet, he *will* get cold. Then, hypothermia, the killer of the unprepared (even in temperatures well above freezing), becomes a very real threat. The only way to warm up in a situation like this is first to get dry. Solution? Avoid getting wet at all costs.

This means carrying a tent on all overnight trips. It may be difficult at first to rationalize this, particularly if it is a sparkling clear morning and daddy's pack already weighs fifty pounds. But any experienced backpacker can cite numerous examples of similarly clear mornings that suddenly have transformed to full-fledged storms by midafternoon.

There are many outstanding backpack tents currently on the market that provide various combinations of good design and strength, yet are lightweight and durable. The features we have found that need particular attention from the point of view of small children are listed here.

Strength and Durability

Every conscientious parent has the instinctive need to provide shelter for his family. Our conscience is at ease on backcountry trips knowing that regardless of how bad the weather may suddenly turn, we have a dry and dependable shelter. For us, complete confidence in our tent as well as our other equipment is essential to our enjoyment of the trip. Thus you want to be certain your tent is constructed of good materials. Ripstop nylon is rapidly becoming a standard fabric on quality tents, but it has a few disadvantages to be mentioned later. Tightly woven cotton or cotton-synthetic blends can also provide outstanding strength and durability although the weight and upkeep is significantly greater. Avoid the bargain basement specials. Many are of poor design and workmanship and are suited only for backyard overnights.

Design

The two factors that will test the design of your tent are rain and wind. If both arrive in force, only the best of tents

Our external frame Draw-Tite, manufactured by Eureka Tent and Awning Co., is quick and easy to set up and requires no pegs or guylines. It is roomy enough inside for two adults, two small children, and, in extenuating circumstances, the family dog.

will meet your expectations. A coated nylon fly is an absolute must if you have to withstand anything more than a passing shower. It must be large enough to completely overlap the tent body yet not droop in any place to come in contact with it. It must be adequately guyed to avoid flapping and thus possible tearing or fraying in high winds. A splash guard extending six or more inches above the ground as well as a nylon-coated floor are standard items on quality tents.

A few reputable tents are available without flies. Their fabric is either very tightly woven or coated nylon. In either case, a ventilation system is designed to eliminate condensing body moisture on the inside of the tent. This is perhaps adequate for one or two inactive adults when a good breeze is blowing, but with two adults and two children with rain outside and no wind, dissipation of body moisture becomes a serious problem.

A porous, breathable, cotton-covered tent with a completely waterproof fly make a good combination even though its total weight is greater than an all-nylon tent. We prefer this because of the restless sleeping habits of our children. If

A rain fly is essential in rainy country. This one is designed to overlap the tent walls so that the tent remains dry even in the hardest rain.

there is even the slightest slope to the tent floor, the boys inevitably respond to gravity and end up at the lowest part of the tent—where moisture is most likely to accumulate. Their down sleeping bags then soak up the condensation. In an unporous tent, this leads to damp, uncomfortable bags and unhappy children.

Equally important is the adequacy of netting at all openings. Your tent must be absolutely bugproof and insectproof. In the various regions of the world where we have backpacked with our children, we have been forced to the conclusion that mosquitoes, black flies, and no-see-ums have a universal and insatiable appetite for tender, young skin. Modern repellents and longsleeved shirts do wonders to alleviate the problem, but in the final analysis, no one will be happy unless refuge can be taken in a well-netted tent. Because kids do tend to roll about during the night, they frequently become exposed around the neck and arms. For that reason, before you turn in, systematically check the high points in your tent with a flashlight for a few stowaway mosquitoes who are looking for an easy meal.

Another aspect of design that is important is the height of your tent. In order to withstand high winds and to avoid unnecessary strain on the tent seams and fabric, a low tent is desirable. It does seem convenient to have a tent high enough to stand up in, and most "family" tents we have seen are built this way. But a tall tent is a pure luxury, at the cost of added weight and an inherent lack of stability. We adhere to the view that a tent is meant primarily to sleep in, and since we do that in the prone position, the few extra feet on top are superfluous. Your tent should be high enough to sit comfortably or even stoop, but if you really have to stand up, step outside to do it.

The last aspect of design worth mentioning is the matter of sufficient floor space for your needs. We have found a floor area measuring 5.5 feet by 7.5 feet to be just adequate for ourselves and the two boys. A bit more area on occasion would have been desirable, like when we once took pity on our eighty-pound Labrador Retriever when he was being devoured by mosquitoes. Since greater floor area (as with greater height) obviously means more weight, a compromise must be reached.

Ease of Setting Up

One of the secrets of successful backpacking with small children is to maintain the maximum possible flexibility in terms of when and where to stop for the day. A quickly erectable tent helps make this possible. An exterior frame tent is well suited for this purpose. It may be set up without stakes, guylines, or trees in literally a few minutes. This is particularly useful above timberline or when an afternoon shower is about to descend, and everybody is ready to stop for the day anyway.

Weight

The total weight of your tent is obviously an important factor. It is discussed last not because it is least important but because once you have decided which features, size, and fabric are necessary for your family's needs, the weight of the tent is determined within a pound or two. It is pointless, in fact dangerous, to carry a three-and-a-half-pound all-nylon tent if it does not give the performance you expect of it. You must have complete confidence in your tent—and you won't if the fabric or the design are less than adequate.

A good quality nylon tent suitable for two adults and two small children will weigh around six to seven pounds including the fly. Its cotton equivalent weighs around eleven to twelve pounds depending on the specific model. The latter amounts to about three tent pounds per person, which is about the maximum you ought to allow.

Sleeping Bags

The acquisition of a quality mountain tent insures that your family will remain dry in any kind of weather. The next step is to insure their warmth, whether it be while waiting out a snowstorm or just sleeping out on a cold night. These two factors, dryness and warmth, are absolutely essential to the maintenance of normal body temperature.

Parents who already own quality down sleeping bags may initially consider the possibility of a communal sleeping arrangement—that is, junior in with mom or dad or both. We tried this one summer with Greg when he was not quite a year old. We were in a splendid mountainous region in southern Norway, and had thoroughly enjoyed this outing with Greg. Having switched him and his kiddie pack back and forth between us during the day, we were looking forward to easing our weary bones down into the lofty folds of our down bags after dinner. The master plan, conceived before the trip, was to have Greg sleep with us. In theory, this seemed reasonable enough. Our two bags when zipped together provide extra roomy quarters, and everyone knows that a small child just does not occupy much space. So we thought. Greg went down immediately after having his bottle, and after enjoying the last flickering coals of our small cooking fire, we joined him. Everyone was soon sound asleep. Around one or two in the morning, Jim awoke to the sensation of a small, damp body pressed tightly against his back. It was Greg, no doubt about it. Jim shifted slightly in an attempt to avoid him, but only a few minutes passed before Greg again occupied the depression created between Jim's body and the foam pad beneath. Each time Jim rolled away, Greg followed relentlessly. Before long, he had us both packed like sardines against one side of the sleeping bag.

Greg, of course, was not the least bothered by the whole affair, particularly with over half the bag in his sole possession. Fearful of rolling onto him if we ever got back to sleep, we repositioned him. In the process we discovered to our dismay that a large part of our beautiful down bag could no longer be occupied with comfort. In expanding his territory, Greg had left a large damp area in his wake. For a one-year-old, it was just a normal night; for his parents, it was a quite sleepless one.

The next night, with an additional pair of plastic pants, a thick cotton sleeper, and a waterproof pad underneath, we tried again. Fortunately for our sleeping bag, the urine treatment of the previous night was avoided. Greg's physical activity, however, was sufficient to wake us several times during the night. Not only did he roll in his sleep, he wriggled. And to add unanticipated variety, he also displayed an incredible repertoire of baby noises ranging from the standard coos to full-fledged snores. All of these apparently went unnoticed at home where he had his own room and crib. But in the close quarters of a sleeping bag, we became quickly convinced this was not the proper way to handle small children when camping.

Not long after this experiment, we became serious about buying Greg a bag of his own. Since our down bags had given us years of dependable service and warmth, it seemed worth the investment to provide him with the same but in a smaller size. We were a bit surprised to find that there were no down bags specially tailored to children available at that time. After poring through several of our favorite catalogs, the closest we could come to what we had in mind was a down-filled foot sack, or "elephant's foot," intended more for emergency bivouacking by adults than for extended use by a child. On the verge of sending in our order, the memory of our urine-soaked down bag returned. An all-down sleeping bag for Greg would not do.

The only recourse was to construct a bag on our own. It soon became an exciting project, for we had hit upon a design that seemed ideally suited for babies or small children

To construct a sleeping bag, set aside a large work space and begin by getting the children involved. This is going to be their very own sleeping bag. Incorporate their ideas and suggestions where feasible.

Lay out the fabric and mark for cutting. Bag of goose down in background holds ½ pound and retails for around $9.00 a pound.

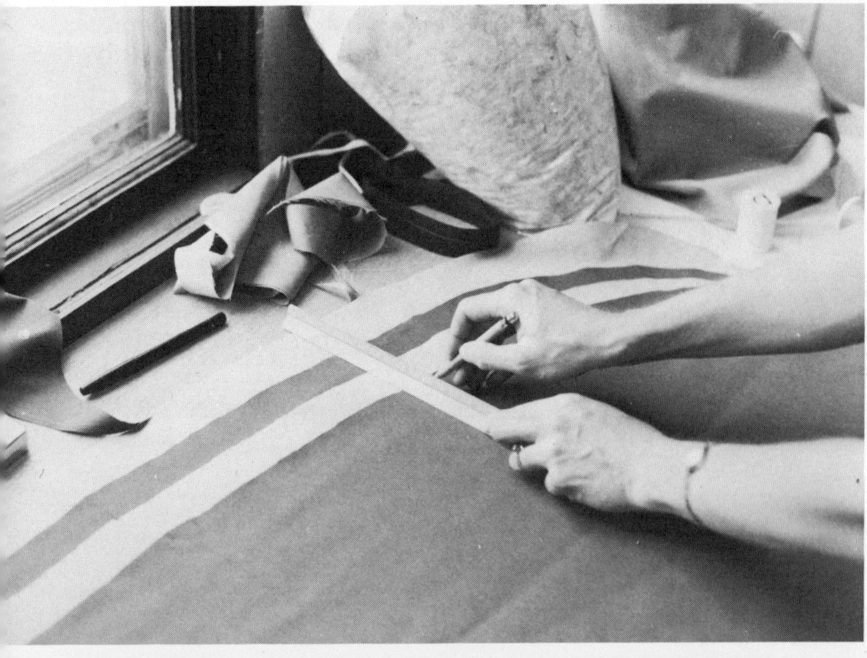

who have nighttime wetting problems. The basic design is simple. There is a top half and a bottom half connected together on three sides by a single, extralong separating zipper. The top half is of boxlike construction and is filled with prime quality goose down for loft and absorbence where it is needed most. The bottom half is filled with Dacron polyester fiberfill. In the event of a nighttime wetting, the bottom half can be easily detached from the top to be rinsed and dried. Dacron polyester has a distinct advantage over down in this respect—it dries far faster. It is also unaffected chemically by urine whereas the delicate fibers of goose down are.

Here is how to go about it. First lay out a work area, preferably a separate sewing room. Then set aside a couple of days to do the job. If you allow the construction to drag on several weeks on a part-time basis, your enthusiasm and the interest of the kids will suffer.

The next step is to plan the bag's dimensions and determine the yardage that will be required. The easiest thing to do is to have the prospective occupant lie prone on the floor in his usual sleeping position. Measure his actual width plus or minus an inch or two and then add six to eight inches on each side for the total width. Then double that dimension for the length. Allow five-eighths-inch on all sides for seams. We made a new bag for Greg when he was four years old with the idea he would use it for at least two or three seasons. The dimensions of the cut fabric were thirty inches by sixty inches.

Whatever fabric you choose, you need two pieces with the above dimensions for a top and bottom lining and two pieces of the same dimensions for the top and bottom covering. The top covering and top lining are then sewn together by a series of cloth baffles running across the width and spaced five to six inches apart. Each strip is three to four inches wide, and for Greg's bag eleven were required to separate the twelve tubes that later were filled with goose down. The material used for lining will also work quite well for these strips.

Sew in the baffles using a regular sewing machine. Cotton-covered Dacron polyester thread gives extra strength to seams and is easy to sew with.

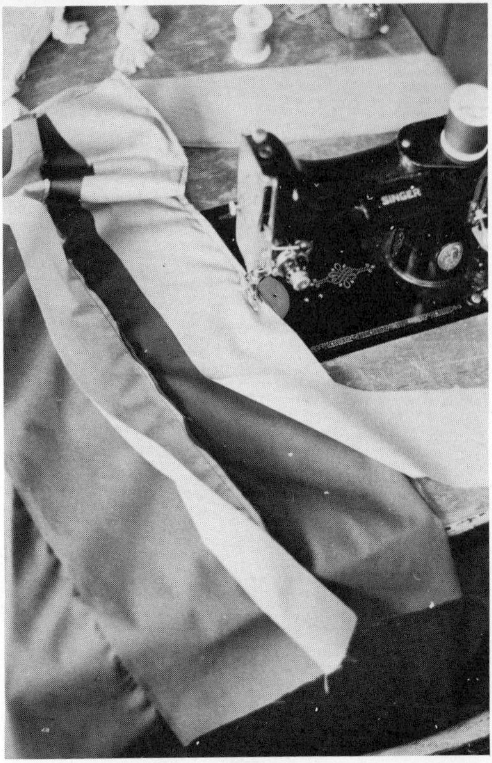

Here the baffles are all sewn into the outer shell and are ready to be sewn to the corresponding inner lining.

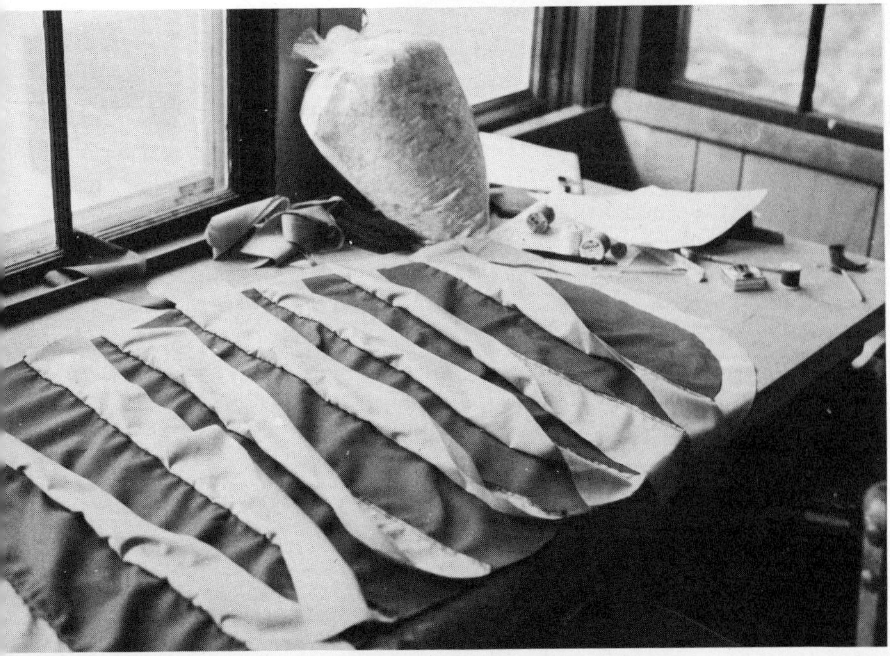

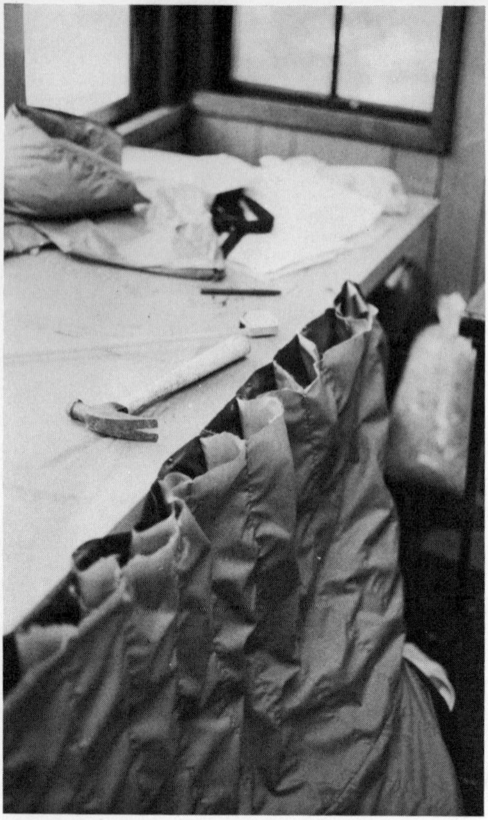

The previous step is completed, and one side and ends of the bag are sewn shut. The bag is now ready for filling with down (top half of bag) and/or Dacron polyester (bottom half of bag). These halves are connected with a full-length separating zipper.

Mark the proper position for each strip with chalk or crayon on the inside surface where it will not show later. You should end up with the top lining and the top cover held together by the appropriate number of cloth strips that run across the width of the bag. The ends of the channels are open at this stage.

The channels are then filled with down and sewn shut at the ends. This is easily accomplished by sewing closed one end of all channels along one side of the bag and then tacking the bag against a table with the open ends up. Then reach into your bag of down and extract one tight handful for each tube. Repeat the operation until each tube is equally full. Then sew closed the open ends. The total amount of down depends on the bag size. Greg's sixty-inch bag described earlier was filled top and bottom with down and took one pound, four ounces total. His first bag when he was two years old took twelve ounces in the top only. The next step is to sew in one-half of an extralong separating zipper all around the outside edge of the top half of the bag.

The entire procedure is then repeated for the bottom half of the bag. But this time the channels are filled with Dacron polyester for a very small child or down for an older child. The other half of the zipper is sewn in, and you are ready to go.

The nice thing about doing your own bag is that there is unlimited opportunity to modify the design and materials to meet your needs. The bag above lacks a down-filled zipper cover to prevent heat loss along the zipper. This can easily be incorporated as can a hood, an extralong dimension, or extra down at the foot or head of the bag.

Because the insulating quality of any sleeping bag depends on the thickness of dead air space between the occupant and his surroundings, the more loft your bag has the warmer you will be. Per unit weight, high quality goose down is unsurpassed as an insulating material. The always dependable dry warmth your down bag provides is not only due to loft but also to the highly absorbent nature of down. The pint or so of perspiration an adult body releases during the course of a normal night would lead to miserable sleeping conditions, indeed, if not for these absorbent qualities. Even though children generally have very good circulation and thus require less loft in a sleeping bag for an equivalent warmth rating, they do need an absorbent insulator to maintain body dryness.

By incorporating Dacron as an insulator in the bottom half of a child's bag, little effective insulation is lost. Compressed down and compressed Dacron have essentially the same insulating value since neither has significant loft beneath one's body.

As for the interior lining, most commercial bags now use ripstop nylon. This is a superb fabric for tents and garments that require great strength yet light weight. But ripstop, because of its very fine weave and synthetic nature, tends to be a bit clammy. This is particularly true on warm nights when the absorbing qualities of down could be more effectively used.

An alternative is Dacron sheath lining, available at any fabric store and at about half the cost of ripstop nylon. The weave is not as tight, yet in our experience is quite downproof. Our own bags are now seven years old, and the Dacron lining has held up extremely well after a full three months' use each of those summers and use as a comforter on our bed at home during the winter months. The less dense weave permits greater breathability, which in turn provides a drier, more comfortable sleeping bag. In addition to the weave, Dacron lining has the advantage of "draping" more effectively than ripstop. That is, Dacron seems to conform to one's body curvature more readily than the somewhat stiffer ripstop. Thus there is less unoccupied air volume that must be heated by a small body.

One final advantage of Dacron is that its greater porosity enables children to breathe easily when snuggled inside. A good test is to try inhaling air through ripstop nylon held tightly over your mouth and then to try it with Dacron sheath lining. When it gets cold at night, our boys usually disappear into the depths of their bags with perhaps only a few tufts of hair showing their presence. We have always been confident of their ability to get an adequate amount of air.

For kids who have grown out of the bed-wetting stage, there are several good sleeping bags available at a range of prices. Nearly every manufacturer of quality mountaineering products markets a foot sack or bivouac bag for emergency adult use. These are filled with up to a pound of goose or duck down and are adequate for children from four and a half to five feet tall. These bags generally have no zippers. The prices range from about $40.00 to $70.00.[1]

[1] All prices are *estimated* on 1975 values. All prices are subject to change without notice.

Specially designed bags for children are now available on the market but are handled by only a few dealers. The North Face Company produces sophisticated down mummy bags (available through Eastern Mountain Sports catalog) for children up to five feet two inches tall. The bag is lined and covered with 1.9 ounce ripstop and is filled with 20 ounces of prime duck down giving a total weight of two pounds and eight ounces. The price is a little over $50.00. Eddie Bauer of Seattle and more recently Minneapolis, now offers their Junior Camper, another goose down bag designed for children up to about four feet seven inches tall. It is a rectangular bag with a sewn-through construction weighing about one and a half pounds. The price is about $40.00.

Recreational Equipment, Inc. now produces a junior version of their well-known McKinley model mummy bag. It is designed for children and small adults under five feet in height. Filling is composed of one and a half pounds of prime duck down enclosed in a nylon taffeta shell. The box-type construction, single nylon zipper, and drawstring at the top are standard features as on the adult McKinley. The total weight is two-and-three-quarter pounds, and the price is about $40.00.

For the more industrious parent, Frostline of Broomfield, Colorado, markets a make-it-yourself kit for a child-sized down bag. A unique feature is its "add-on" construction that allows the addition of down-filled sections to the length of the bag as your child grows older. The basic bag will accommodate a child up to four feet tall. A single extension will add another twelve inches to the bag's length. The bag is filled with prime duck down giving an average loft of two and a half inches. Total weight without add-on section is two pounds, ten ounces. The price for the kit is slightly over $30.00. We have observed a few of Frostline's adult sleeping bag kits in construction from start to finish. If the directions are as explicit for their child's bag, it can be assembled by anyone who can use a sewing machine.

Several Dacron-filled sleeping bags are available in children's sizes. As mentioned, we do not recommend them for

Catalog Suppliers of Children's Sleeping Bags and Packs

Sleeping Bags

Eddie Bauer
P.O. Box 3700
Seattle, Washington
98124

Camp 7, Inc. (foot sack)
3235 Prairie
Boulder, Colorado 80301

Comfy, Division of Olin
310 First Ave. South
Seattle, Washington
98104

Eastern Mountain Sports
(North Face bags)
1041 Commonwealth Ave.
Boston, Massachusetts
02215

Frostline Kits
Dept. C, P.O. Box 589
Broomfield, Colorado
80020

Gerry, Division of
Outdoor Sports, Inc.
5450 North Valley
Highway
Denver, Colorado 80216

Holubar, Carikits
Box 7
Boulder, Colorado 80302

Recreational Equipment,
Inc.
1525 11th Ave.
Seattle, Washington
98122

Sierra Designs
Mail Order Dept.
4th and Addison Streets
Berkeley, California
94710

Packs

Alpine Designs
6185 East Arapahoe
P.O. Box 3407
Boulder, Colorado 80303

Camp Trails
P.O. Box 14500
Phoenix, Arizona 85063

Eastern Mountain Sports
1041 Commonwealth Ave.
Boston, Massachusetts
02215

Gerry, Division of
Outdoor Sports, Inc.
5450 North Valley
Highway
Denver, Colorado 80216

backpacking purposes. An exception may be du Pont's new Dacron Polyester Fiberfill II. It is designed especially for sleeping bags and is apparently much improved over their previous fiberfill insulation. The material is advertised to have a very low fiber-to-fiber friction level, which accounts for its similarity in performance to natural down. Comfy Products, a division of Olin, Seattle, Washington, now markets a child's bag insulated with Fiberfill II. It is their Wasatch Jr. model with one pound of filling in a seventy-three-inch bag. Its suggested comfort temperature, however, is only 30° F. This is a marginal comfort rating for many mountainous regions of the country even during the summer months.

We well remember an outing to the Mojave Desert, in California, with Greg and Chris when they were three and a half and one and a half years of age, respectively. The occasion was a geologic field trip attended by thirty adults and a few children. In February, the desert can be warm and delightful, especially when the early spring wildflowers appear. But it can also show its darker side with subfreezing temperatures and high winds. Such were the conditions on this particular outing. On our first night out, the thermometer read 10° F. amid the cactus and sand. A thirty-mile-per-hour wind served not only to blow sand into everything in camp but also chilled everyone right to the bone. Greg and Chris snuggled into their fluffy down sleeping bags right after dinner and slept warm and sound through the night. Most of the adults stood around a roaring campfire in an attempt to warm up before turning in. About half of the group had Dacron bags, and most survived for only a few hours before seeking refuge in a nearby motel. The remaining members of our group had down bags and managed quite well.

Foam Pads

An adequate insulation beneath your child's bag is as important to maintaining his warmth as it is to maintaining your own. The easiest way to provide for his needs is to purchase an adult hip-length pad or simply construct a child-sized pad. Ensolite is an ideal material because of its light weight, insulating qualities, and compactness. It can also be easily cut to whatever size you desire. We have successfully used open cell foam covered on top with absorbent cotton poplin and beneath with coated nylon. Such pads must be thicker than closed cell pads to provide equivalent insulation because of their greater compressibility. The added thickness, however, provides greater protection from the inevitable pinecones, twigs, and rocks that always remain beneath the tent even after the most diligent search. An open cell pad and cotton cover have the advantage of providing a more absorbent combination, which means a drier and warmer sleeping arrangement.

In our experience the only problem with foam pads is keeping Greg and Chris on them. Both boys are restless sleepers and tend to roll or scoot off their pads unless we take special care in arranging them. On a few occasions we have been awakened by a cry of discomfort coming from an unpadded corner of the tent. By choosing a flat tent site and by covering the unpadded area with clothes and packs, we end up with a wall-to-wall carpeting that solves the problem.

An alternative solution to the problem is to sew a special pocket onto the lower half of a child's bag. Into this you can fit an Ensolite pad, thus eliminating the problem of separated pads and sleeping bags. The pad should not be permanently sewn in if you plan to stuff the bag or remove the pad for washing purposes.

Under no condition would we seriously consider using air mattresses in place of foam pads. Not only are they less comfortable and more difficult to sleep on but the mere thought of inflating and deflating four mattresses for our family is exhausting.

Packs

As mentioned earlier in the chapter, there is important psychological value to having packs for small children. Both Greg and Chris had their very own packs when only two years old. In both cases, the pack was an all-nylon version made by Gerry Products and weighed only a few ounces. It was quite adequate, though, to hold those all-important trail snacks and hard candies.

When Greg turned four years old, he carried an all-nylon pack with an adjustable aluminum frame. The combination is a Jan Sport model that retails in the $20.00 range. Its major advantage is that Greg can continue to use the frame as he grows. Good quality packs will not wear out in a few years and thus make good hand-me-downs.

First-Aid Kit

A good first-aid kit is essential on any backpacking trip. It must contain all of the normal items for adult needs and in addition some extra items specially intended for children. If properly assembled, it will provide for the majority of minor accidents and ailments you are likely to encounter in a wilderness situation. There are no ready-made kits on the market that will be ideally suited to your needs, but there are several that provide a compact container and the basic ingredients for a good kit. We chose a flexible plastic model measuring 3″ × 5″ × 2″ and that now contains the following:

Chris's pack is all nylon. It carries his down jacket and the lemon drop supply. Greg's larger pack has an adjustable aluminum frame.

Item	*Size*	*Quantity*	*Purpose*
Adhesive bandage strips	¾″	20	minor cuts
Adhesive bandage strips	¼″	10	minor cuts
Adhesive butterflies	¼″	6	closing open wounds
Adhesive tape	½″	10 yds.	holding bandages
Sterile gauze bandage	1″	10 yds.	dressing
Sterile gauze pad	4″ x 4″	3	dressing, severe bleeding
Aspirin (adult)	5 g	10	pain, colds
Aspirin (child)	1-¼ g	20	fussiness, pain, colds
Gelatin sticks	2″ x ¼″	6	constipation
Lip salve	2″	1	cold sores
Lip balm [2]	2″	1	chapped lips
Tweezers	3″	1	splinters
Needle	2″	1	splinters
Razor blade (single-edged)	1″	1	cutting tool
First-aid cream	3″	1	burns, scrapes
Antiseptic soap	4″	1	sterile cleansing of wounds
Ammonia inhalants	1″	2	restore consciousness
Elastic bandage	2″ x 3′	1	sprained ankle
Moleskin		1 pkt	blisters
First-aid manual [3]	23 pp.	1	reference
Matches (kitchen)	2″	10	sterilization, fire, light
Sunburn lotion [2]	4″	1	sunburn

[2] Preventative medicine, use freely each day.

[3] *Mountaineering First Aid,* copyright © 1960, 1967 by The Mountaineers, P.O. Box 122, Seattle, Washington 98111.

Item	*Size*	*Quantity*	*Purpose*
Penicillin		1 pkt	infection
Thermometer	child	1	temperature
Snakebite kit (in snake country only)			
Instant cold compress	2″ x 3″	1	bites, headache, stings

Nearly all of these items can be obtained at your local drugstore. Most will be prepackaged, and you will want to leave adhesive bandage boxes and the like at home so that a more compact kit will be possible.

We have found that aside from the normal array of scratches, sunburn, and sore muscles, major injuries and sickness are rare. Wilderness terrain is essentially germ-free and actually a very healthy place to live. In the two summers we have spent with the boys in Alaska, neither of them has even had a sniffle. Despite the rain and cold and persistent exposure to the elements, they remained in perfect health. It was only upon return to the populated cities that we were again exposed to the everyday viruses and germs.

There are several precautions that can be taken prior to your trip that will minimize the chances of major sickness. First, see your family doctor and tell him your plans. Have each person in the family checked for normal blood pressure. Some medical authorities suspect that the rarified air of high mountainous regions can have an adverse effect on very small infants. Furthermore, if anyone in the family has a recurring ailment, be sure to include appropriate treatment for it in your first-aid kit. Lastly, if your doctor recommends that because of ill health you should not plan an extended backpacking trip, take his advice and stay home. The backcountry is for healthy people who want to remain healthy.

While at your doctor's office, seek his advice on obtaining

penicillin for combating infections that you or your children might incur. He may have additional suggestions as well that may require his written prescription. Be sure everyone has a current tetanus inoculation.

Another precaution well worth taking is a matter of first-aid education. The American Red Cross offers short courses on emergency first aid in every major city in the country. Read a good first-aid manual from cover to cover so you will know what to do in the event of an emergency. There is not much point in lugging along a complete manual on your trip because there is usually no time in an emergency to thumb through a thick volume. We carry the compact booklet referred to on pages 67 and 68; it summarizes first-aid treatment for the most common emergencies.

The last precaution, which is perhaps most important of all, is to use common sense and good judgment as preventative medicine. See to it that your children dress properly with hats and sunglasses on bright days, and that they stay warm and dry on cold, wet days. A liberal dose of suntan lotion and regular applications of lip balm will prevent unnecessary discomfort. Make regular checks for tender spots on feet before blisters appear. With proper socks and well-tied shoes, these can be prevented.

You can do a lot by anticipating potential trouble. Hold hands when crossing snowbanks, and particularly when crossing streams. Learn to recognize and avoid poison oak, poison ivy, poison sumac, and nettles. (See Chapter 7 for more on potential hazards.)

Lastly remember that everyone in the family is out to have an enjoyable time, so don't overdo it. If your children are irritable and are reluctant to proceed further on the trail, they may be tired and ready for a nap. Outdoor living day and night for an extended period of time is a substantial change for all of us, and your system must have adequate time to adjust. So take it easy, avoiding overexertion that could lower resistance.

5

Small Appetites Become Large

THE MOST IMPORTANT FACTOR contributing to the success of family backpacking trips, as far as our children are concerned, is food. The combination of hiking and mountain air perks up appetites to an uncanny degree. By midafternoon we find ourselves already contemplating dinner. The conversation seems to become more and more centered around food the closer we get to the evening campsite.

How Much Food?

Whether you are planning a trip for two days or twelve, you are already committed to a fixed, minimum weight for basic equipment and clothes. The only important remaining variable is food. How much to take (and, therefore, how long you can travel) will depend on the maximum weight you can carry comfortably. A careful choice of foods, however, will prolong one's ventures into the backcountry. Our experience has been that seven full days of food plus an extra day's rations for emergency use only, is about all that two adults and two small children can readily carry. There is one consolation, though: Your pack will grow lighter as each day passes. For your first dinner you may even include treats you would not normally carry, such as fresh meat, a cucumber, fresh fruit, or a carefully wrapped tomato. The amount of fresh goodies you bring will be directly proportional to the strength of your back!

If the fixed minimum weight for equipment and clothes is fifty to fifty-five pounds, and eighty pounds is a comfortable load for two adults, you have about twenty-five to thirty pounds left for food.

What Kind of Food?

It is important that meals be nutritious, appetizing, and satisfying. On top of that, they must be reasonably lightweight. That is a tall order for any menu. By experimenting at home and planning ahead you can satisfy these demands.

At home we eat as much natural, fresh food as possible. This is what we prefer, but this will vary from family to family. Whatever your eating habits, they will require some compromise on a backpacking trip. Obviously, one cannot carry enough fresh food for even a weekend without exceeding reasonable weight and space limits.

Canned foods are eliminated from serious consideration. Their weight consists primarily of water, and as there is normally an abundance of it in most mountainous areas, why bother? Besides, the can symbolizes in our minds one of the undesirable elements we want to get away from by backpacking. Partially burned cans in old fire rings are unsightly and do not add to our enjoyment of the wilderness.

It is most sensible then to rely mainly on dried foods, either dehydrated or freeze-dried. Which dry foods you take is a very subjective decision. We have tried several different

There is never a problem getting a volunteer to clean out the pudding pot. Rocks are a good place to cook and eat because it is easy to clean up afterward.

kinds. Some taste better than others. Some have more preservatives. Some have more packaging. And some take less time to prepare. Certain brands are more expensive, and others have more ample servings. All these factors have to be considered.

We have found it helpful to try several different brands and types of dry food at home before a trip. Then we can determine which ones we prefer, which ones fill us up, and how long the ones we like take to prepare, keeping in mind that it will take longer for things to cook at higher elevations.

It is only by prior experimentation that you can evaluate which foods will work for your family. On one of our trips we met a couple with two children, aged eight and ten. The whole family was satisfied at each meal with a two-man freeze-dried entree. They were all lean of build and simply did not eat very much. Our children, who were only half their children's ages, had much larger appetites. We take a four-man freeze-dried entree and supplement it with soup, drinks, and dessert.

If you find some freeze-dried foods bland and boring, try adding some of your favorite spices. For us, basil or thyme enhances most casseroles. Cinnamon and nutmeg really jazz up vanilla pudding and applesauce.

Entire prepackaged freeze-dried meals can be purchased, but this gets expensive and limits choice greatly. We prefer to buy a freeze-dried vegetable and meat and add our own casserole ingredients or, as mentioned before, supplement a freeze-dried entree with soup, drinks, and dessert. In this way you can save money, and you have the satisfaction of assembling your own menus to your own family's tastes and appetites. You also have better control over quantities and quality of individual food items.

What about Nutrition?

You may wonder, and with reason, whether your family can get enough nutrition out of a diet lacking in fresh foods. To check this out we asked several freeze-dried food manufacturers about the caloric and protein content of their products.

For backpacking purposes, protein is probably the most important constituent of the diet because it produces energy throughout the day—and backpacking requires a great deal of energy.

Table I shows the number of grams of protein required per day for children and adults. The numbers are based on average requirements under usual environmental conditions. They should be considered as minimal figures in view of the physical and emotional levels of activity attained on backpacking trips.

TABLE I
Recommended Daily Dietary Allowances [1]

Age (*yrs.*)	*Weight* (*lbs.*)	*Height* (*in.*)	*Energy* (*cal.*)	*Protein* (*g.*)
1–3	28	34	1,300	23
4–6	44	44	1,800	30
7–10	66	54	2,400	36
23–50 (f)	128	65	2,000	46
23–50 (m)	154	69	2,700	56

[1] Food and Nutrition Board, National Academy of Sciences, National Research Council Recommendation, Revised 1973.

Freeze-dried foods, like their fresh equivalents, have a wide range of caloric and protein content. A menu of freeze-dried foods for one day that is fairly typical and would please most children is listed in Table II. Purchased in four-man portions at a cost under $10.00, it has a daily total of 47 grams of protein and 2,354 calories (per adult serving). But note that the minimum adult protein requirements are 46 grams for a 23–50-year-old woman and 56 grams for a 23–50-year-old man; the caloric requirements are 2,000 and 2,700 calories, respectively. In the menu given, therefore, the caloric intake is adequate for the female but not for the male. The protein content is barely adequate for the female and inadequate for the male. What about a four-year-old? He's getting all his requirements, providing you can figure out a way to stuff over five pounds of solid and liquid into his stomach in three sittings. But this is almost impossible.

Table I shows that a four-to-six-year old requires only 200 calories per day less than an adult female, yet his stomach is much smaller. At each meal a young child with a good appetite will eat about half of an adult serving. This reduces his protein and caloric intake to approximately 24 grams and 1,200 calories. Therefore, alas, for a child, a totally freeze-dried menu of three meals a day is inadequate. The solution? Supplement the freeze-dried foods with fresh, protein-

TABLE II

Sample Freeze-Dried Menu [2] *(per serving)*

	Reconstituted Weight (oz.)	*Protein (g.)*	*Calories*
Breakfast			
instant applesauce	4	trace	128
pancake mix	5	7.2	310
syrup	2	trace	140
cocoa	12	5.7	187
	23	12.9	765
Lunch			
peanut butter	1.5	trace	7.8
jelly	1.5	trace	34
Pilot biscuits	2.5	4.0	192
freeze-dried ice cream	1.25	3.4	184
lemon-lime drink	12.0	0.1	196
	18.75	7.5	613.8
Dinner			
Vegetable stew with beef	10.0	10.9	230
tomato noodle soup	8.0	3.9	101
dumplings	4.0	7.7	424
butterscotch pudding	5.0	3.9	124
pineapple-orange drink	12.0	0.1	196
	39.0	26.5	1,075
Totals	5.04 pounds	46.9 grams	2,453.8 calories

[2] Data obtained from Richmoor freeze-dried food nutritional guide.

enriched foods and see to it that your small children eat often. For an adult, a freeze-dry diet is not ideal, but it will probably not do any harm. How to do this will be discussed under each meal heading.

In all fairness to freeze-dried food companies, it should be stated that the above example is on the low end nutritionally of what they offer. There are much more nutritious products on the market. But you do have to check the ingredients and the nutritional information on the label. If such information is not listed, write to the company in question. Your family's welfare depends on it!

It is also true that the more protein in a freeze-dried food, the more expensive it is. When you make up your own menus, meals can turn out to be less expensive and more appetizing than an entirely freeze-dried meal.

We must also be concerned about vitamins in our menus. Although the freeze-dried manufacturers are working on the vitamin content of their products there is little specific information about this at the present time. Therefore supplementing the freeze-dried menus becomes important not only to increase the protein intake but to insure an adequate vitamin intake as well.

Vitamin A is needed for good vision and for healthy skin and mucous membranes. Children ages four to six need 2,500 units, daily.[3] The easiest way of supplying this is to pack along dry *whole* milk. A cup of whole milk (reconstituted) contains 290 units of vitamin A whereas a cup of skim milk contains none.[4] Additional vitamin A can be obtained from cheese and dry apricots in lunches.

Vitamin C is needed for the formation and maintenance of connective tissues in the body and for healthy skin and gums.[5] A child's minimum daily requirement of vitamin C is 50 milligrams.[6] It can be provided by packing along a for-

[3] Food and Nutrition Board.

[4] Adelle Davis, *Let's Eat Right to Keep Fit* (New York: Harcourt Brace Jovanovich, rev. ed. 1970), p. 276.

[5] Davis, *Let's Eat Right to Keep Fit,* pp. 122–124.

[6] Food and Nutrition Board.

tified instant juice. There are several on the market that have vitamin C and sometimes vitamin A added. The Tang label claims that 16.5 grams or two rounded teaspoons contain 405 percent of a child's daily requirement of vitamin C and 44 percent of vitamin A. Vitamin C is also found in dry apricots but not in raisins.

The B vitamins help the body through stress situations.[7] On backpacking trips they can be obtained via the wheat germ in biscuits and pancakes and granola, the brewer's yeast in trail bars and granola, and in sunflower seeds and nuts. Iron is present, by the way, in foods rich in B vitamins.

If you are worried about getting enough vitamins while out in the wilderness, the easiest way to relieve your mind is probably to bring along multiple vitamin tablets. This is something that is going to vary from family to family. Personally, we find taking pills too much trouble. Of course, if anyone in the family is on a restricted diet for medical reasons, you should always consult the doctor before making up your menus.

Looking at Some Satisfying Meals

Breakfast

In our family, breakfast is a necessary meal. We really can't think of setting off without a good breakfast, preferably hot. At the same time, it is difficult to carry fresh, nourishing foods for breakfast. Eggs break, pork sausage spoils, syrup is heavy, there is no toaster. There are many ways of getting around these obstacles, but they do take some preplanning.

First of all forget the toast. Bread is a poor traveler, metamorphosing after a few hours into thousands of crumbs. If you want bread, try a biscuit mix either prepackaged in one meal amounts, or for more nutrition make your own mix with

[7] Davis, *Let's Eat Right to Keep Fit*, p. 68.

Freshly caught rainbow trout provide a fine protein supplement to your wilderness diet.

lots of wheat germ for a nutty flavor.[8] Biscuit mix rises surprisingly well in a light fry pan over a fire or stove. The fry pan need not even be covered.

Freeze-dried and dehydrated eggs are surprisingly good. Try several brands to see which is the most appealing. Don't worry about the lumps when you are reconstituting them; they somehow dissolve in the fry pan. If they still taste papery the addition of bits of cheddar cheese and some onion will do wonders for the taste and will boost the protein intake too.

If you are going to be near a lake or stream, take along something to flour the trout. We like to use a mixture of flour and wheat germ in a plastic bag. To fry the trout we prefer margarine. (We have never had margarine spoil at high eleva-

[8] Recipes at end of chapter.

tions. It gets quite cool at night, and during the day it is buried in the pack insulated from the heat.) Many brands come in convenient one-half pound plastic tubs that will not leak in your pack. Fish and biscuits are a favorite hot breakfast, and sticks with us long into the morning.

Pancake mixes can be purchased in small packets as can biscuit mixes. Some need only water, others must have milk; reconstituted dried milk is fine, but you must take this into account when planning. We prefer to make our own pancake mix. It is the same as the biscuit mix with more milk added. Our boys adore pancakes, so to please them we make sure we have at least one pancake breakfast for each trip. Syrup is carried in a small, polyethylene bottle containing four fluid ounces or one half-cup. True, we don't drown our pancakes in syrup. If you must have lots of syrup you may decide it isn't worth carrying.

One of the most nutritious breakfasts we eat is granola with

Pancakes over our Svea stove provide variety to our breakfast menu. They taste especially good on rainy mornings like this one when we took shelter beneath a tree.

milk. It is a natural blend of grains, oil, and honey that is easily made at home. It is packed with protein. A one-cup serving provides sixteen grams of protein, and a cup of milk brings the total to twenty-three. Another advantage of granola is that nothing has to be cooked. We sometimes reserve it for wet mornings when starting up a fire or the stove would be difficult.

Cooked oatmeal or wheat flakes, to which can be added reconstituted milk, cinnamon, brown sugar, wheat germ, and raisins, makes a delicious and nutritious meal. Likewise, uncooked cereal flakes can be premixed at home with the above named ingredients and *dry* milk for a speedy breakfast in camp where all you have to do is add boiling water and stir a minute. These cereal breakfasts are so filling we don't plan anything else with them except for the juice and hot beverage.

It is important not to be in a terrible rush in the morning. Our boys are ready to hike if they have time to eat a good breakfast and time afterward to play as they wish. We usually wake up around 7:00 and take a full two hours to get dressed, cook, eat, clean up, and break camp. After 9:00 or so we are ready to go, and so are the boys.

Here is an example of what would be in a breakfast bag for a six-day trip:

- 6 small plastic bags containing one-half-cup Tang each (6 quarts reconstituted)
- 1 small poly bottle of one-half-cup freeze-dried coffee (2 cups each per day)
- 12 packets of instant cocoa
- 1 small poly bottle of oil
- 1 one-half-pound tub of margarine
- 1 small poly bottle syrup
- 1 plastic bag with 2 cups of fish breading mixture
- 2 plastic bags with 2 cups biscuit or pancake mix
- 6 quart packages instant dry whole milk
- 1 plastic bag with 4 cups of granola

1 plastic bag with 4 cups of instant hot breakfast
1 plastic bag with 2 cups of uncooked oatmeal
1 plastic bag with brown sugar, cinnamon, wheat germ, and raisins
1 plastic bag with freeze-dried egg, potato, and meat (prepacked)

In the following table is an illustration of the caloric and protein content of the above listed breakfasts:

TABLE III

Caloric and Protein Count in Trail Breakfasts (per serving) [9]

	Ingredients	*Calories*	*Protein (in grams)*
#1	granola	400	16
	milk, powdered, whole, 1 cup [10]	125	7
	instant juice	61	trace
	Total	586	23
#2	instant hot oatmeal with raisins, wheat germ, etc.[11]	360	17
	instant juice	61	trace
	Total	421	17
#3	Freeze-dried eggs	122	11
	bacon bar	100	7.5
	dry hash brown potatoes	120	1.5
	instant juice	61	trace
	Total	403	20.0
#4	trout, 3 oz.	170	20
	homemade biscuit mix (2)	260	8
	2 pats margarine	100	—
	instant juice	61	trace
	Total	591	28

TABLE III (*continued*)

Caloric and Protein Count in Trail Breakfasts (per serving) [9]

	Ingredients	*Calories*	*Protein (in grams)*
#5	buckwheat pancakes with wheat germ (4 cakes)	250	10
	2 pats margarine	100	—
	4 tablespoons syrup	200	—
	cocoa	235	8
	instant juice	61	trace
	Total	846	18

[9] Sources for calories and proteins: Davis, *Let's Eat Right to Keep Fit,* tables of food composition, pp. 276–303. Richmoor Foods "Consumer Menu Planner Nutritional Guide."

[10] Reconstituted.

[11] This breakfast contains approximately the same nutritional value as the cooked oatmeal breakfast, having the same ingredients.

More protein and calories are added to each of the above breakfasts with a cup of milk, as seen in the granola breakfast, as well as in the pancake breakfast.

Lunch

Lunch is definitely our heaviest meal to pack. It consists of natural proteins, fats, sugars, and carbohydrates. The body develops a good appetite by noon, and with a few more miles to go for that evening campsite, it really needs refueling. The lunch menu has always been basically the same with variations on flavor only. We find it very satisfying and never get tired of it.

Specifically, lunch always includes some kind of dry bread or crackers, such as crisp bread, flat bread, or similar starch that has something in it in addition to white flour. We are big cheese eaters and have at least an ounce apiece. We prefer natural, unprocessed types such as cheddar, swiss, and monterey jack. We have found that all travel well, and like the margarine they do not spoil. The children enjoy them. Dry salami is also included, or some kind of beef jerky. Nuts, sunflower seeds, or soynuts are tasty and add a great deal of protein. The meal is finished off with some kind of dry fruit, as raisins, apricots, or apples, and something sweet such as homemade cookies or high protein candy bars purchased at a health food store. An instant drink such as lemonade washes everything down. If we are in camp then we might heat up water for some soup, but if we are on the trail, we are usually too warm for anything hot to drink.

After such a substantial lunch it is important to let the stomach digest it all before hurrying back to the hiking. We find the hour after lunch spent relaxing is most necessary for all of us. Oftentimes fish for the evening meal has been caught during this break.

As the lunch is so large, sometimes part of it is eaten for a snack later on in the afternoon. As will be seen by the following table, the protein intake is enormous if everything is eaten.

TABLE IV

Caloric and Protein Count in Trail Lunches (per serving) [12]

Items	*Calories*	*Proteins (in grams)*
dry bread, 4 pieces	200	4
cheese, Swiss, 1 oz.	105	7
salami, ¼″ x 4″	250	14
dry fruit, ½ cup	240	3
peanuts, ⅓ cup *or*	290	13
sunflower seeds, ½ cup	280	12
homemade trail bars (2)	200	4
instant drink, 8 oz.	100 (approx.)	trace
Total	1665	57

[12] See note #9.

Snacks

Most children, and adults too, enjoy a midmorning or midafternoon snack, especially when they are busy outside for extended periods of time. A nutritious pick-me-up can be just what is needed to make that last half-mile to the lake for the evening campsite. Children, even more than adults, need extra chances to eat protein-rich foods on backpacking trips. Little stomachs fill up fast, and you want them filling up on quality food.

High energy snack foods can be made at home prior to the trip. Most cookies crumble easily, but we found one that didn't that is made with honey instead of refined sugar and is quite nutritious and delicious.

Dried fruit makes a good trail snack. Kids love it, it keeps well, and it promotes regularity. Because of its last attribute, it should be used with moderation. Three or four dried apricots, for example, were enough for our two-year-old per day, when lots of juice drinks were being consumed.

Nuts and sunflower seeds are good snack items. The only problem is that very small children might choke on them. They have to be told to chew them up carefully. Or you could chop the nuts and put them into bars. It definitely helps to take a nut snack when you have lots of water handy as they do make you thirsty.

It is helpful to have a special place just for snack foods that is always easily accessible. A child can carry the day's snack foods in his small pack. It's a little chore, but a necessary one, so the child feels he is really helping.

Sometimes you are in between rest stops, low on water, the snack has already been devoured, and the children say they are both hungry and thirsty. What then? This is the time for a piece of hard candy. Obviously you don't want to get your kids used to having candy all the time, but in such situations it can be a godsend. It gives extra energy and keeps the mouth moist as you suck. Lemon drops are our favorite. On one hot, dusty, long traverse between two lakes we found we went through five drops apiece. They made the difference between an inconvenient lack of water and a real, discomforting thirst.

Dinner

It is imperative that everyone be well-fed after an active, outdoor day. Our children have never slept so well as after a day of exercise, fresh air, and a satisfying dinner. Often the boys would be ravenous by 4:00 P.M., which means planning to stop in time to avoid the ill tempers that stem from hungry stomachs and overtiredness. We usually try to wrap up our hiking by 3:00 or 4:00 in the afternoon, so there is adequate time for play and preparing dinner.

Soup is the first order of business. Instant soup mix needing only boiling water poured into cups is quick and easy to make. The children enjoy drinking warm soup while the rest of the meal is being prepared. The pot used for heating water for soup is then available for the main course, or for presoaking an entree if so required.

The main course can be a freeze-dried affair or one of your own concoction that has been assembled and packaged at home. Freeze-dried vegetables are tasty and can be served separately or mixed into the main dish. Freeze-dried meats can be purchased separately and combined with noodles or rice plus an instant soup or gravy mix of your own choosing.

Dinners can be made more protein-rich by adding freshly caught trout to the menu, by adding cheese to a freeze-dried casserole, and by adding a pudding made with milk. Freeze-dried entrees vary greatly in their protein content. Even using the same brand, the protein content can vary twenty grams among various dinners. The point is to know the protein content of each entree you are considering so that you can add protein where necessary to round out the meal. For example, if the fishing is good one day, that is the time to get out the instant mashed potatoes and to save the chili with beans (thirty-four grams of protein per serving)[13] for a fishless evening.

The beverage usually depends on the weather, but even on a cool evening, hot soup is usually salty and can make children very thirsty in the middle of the night. We always include a cold drink mix to quench thirst and to replenish body fluids lost during the day.

We like to include vegetables in each dinner somewhere. For the first night out you may want to pack something fresh—cucumbers, tomatoes, carrots. Some freeze-dried entrees have quite a few vegetables in them, or freeze-dried vegetables can be added to your own concoctions. We have found the freeze-dried carrots, for example, to be especially tasty.

Taking along fresh meat for the first dinner on the trail is also a possibility, but because of the danger of spoilage, you must consider how hot a day it is apt to be and how long you plan to be on the trail before dinner. On several of our extended trips into the backcountry, we have set off on the trail after lunch. This saves the weight of lunch and assures a relatively short hike on the first day out. Fresh meat and other perishables placed deep into a pack remain surprisingly well insulated for several hours. We have successfully kept freshly caught trout from morning until dinner in the same manner.

We routinely mix a quart of whole, dried milk with the dinner preparation so the children can have as much as they want and so we will have it ready for cooking if needed. The extra can be put into a toddler's bottle for use during the night if necessary or for use in the morning on cereal.

Dessert is a pleasant way to end a meal. It is also a good way to round off the protein count or the vitamin count of the day's food intake. If the day has been a little low in protein, a pudding can be served. If vitamin C has been lacking serve applesauce or some other fruit dessert. It is amazing how

[13] Richmoor nutritional guide.

many instant desserts there are to choose from, both in a supermarket and from a freeze-dried food list.

To sum up, dinner for us always includes a hot soup, a cold drink, a main course with a vegetable, and a dessert. Here are some sample menus for a family of two adults and two children on a six-day trip (soups are all instant):

TABLE V

Caloric and Protein Count in Trail Dinners (per serving) [14]

	Ingredients	*Calories*	*Protein (in grams)*
#1	cream of mushroom soup	200	7
	fresh hamburger	245	21
	cucumber and tomato salad	15	—
	butterscotch pudding (cooked)	124	4
	strawberry drink	200	—
	Total	784	32
#2	tomato noodle soup	101	4
	freeze-dried beef casserole w/ carrots and noodles	289	15
	instant applesauce	128	—
	grape drink	200	—
	Total	718	19
#3	vegetable beef soup	78	4
	chicken rice casserole	283	14
	with peas	46	3
	chocolate pudding	124	4
	lemonade drink	200	—
	Total	731	25
#4	French onion soup	59	2
	instant mashed potatoes	178	5
	fresh trout, 3 oz.	170	20
	string beans	17	1

TABLE V (*continued*)
Caloric and Protein Count in Trail Dinners (per serving)[14]

	Ingredients	*Calories*	*Protein (in grams)*
	2 pats margarine	100	trace
	instant apple compote	274	1
	fruit punch drink	200	—
	Total	998	29
#5	chicken rice soup	139	5
	freeze-dried pork chops	147	18
	hash-brown potatoes	120	2
	freeze-dried peas and carrots	57	2
	instant Jello	268	7
	lime drink	200	—
	Total	931	34
#6	beef bouillon	24	5
	freeze-dried beef stroganoff	381	19
	freeze-dried corn	59	2
	banana creme pudding	124	4
	raspberry drink	200	—
	Total	788	30

[14] See note #9.

Pounds and Ounces

It is important to see how much individual food items weigh so you can estimate the total weight you will be carrying. It is only by getting everything together and weighing each item that you will really know how heavy your food supplies are. Once you have added everything up, you can decide if everything you have included is necessary. You may choose to eliminate the fresh dinner, for example. It depends on what you are used to carrying and how much you feel like carrying. Food for us four for six days comes to about thirty pounds. Here is how the meals break down weight-wise:

Breakfast Bag:

6	plastic bags of Tang (½ cup each)	16.0 oz.
1	plastic bag of freeze-dried coffee	2.0
12	packets instant cocoa	12.0
1	cup oil in small poly bottle	7.5
1	tub margarine	8.0
¾	cup syrup in small poly bottle	8.0
2	cups breading mix in plastic bag	8.0
6	quart packets dry milk	19.2
2	cups pancake mix in plastic bag	8.0
2	cups biscuit mix in plastic bag	8.0
4	cups granola in plastic bag	16.0
4	cups hot oatmeal breakfast in plastic bag	14.2
2	cups uncooked oatmeal in plastic bag	5.5
1½	cups cereal topping	6.0
	freeze-dried eggs, bacon, and hash browns	13.0
		151.4 or 9 lbs. 7 oz.

Lunch Bag:

2	boxes crackers	20.0 oz.
2	packages cheese	24.0
2	sticks salami	24.0

3 small packages sunflower seeds	12.0
3 packages dry fruit	24.0
cookies	24.0
6 quart drink mixes	20.0
	148.0 or 9 lbs. 4 oz.

Snack Bag:

lemon drops	8.0 oz.
pemmican bars	16.0
peanuts	8.0
	32.0 or 2 lbs.

Dinner Bag:

6 quart drink mixes	20.0 oz.
fresh hamburger and vegetables, soup, pudding	37.7
freeze-dried beef casserole with carrots, soup, instant applesauce	15.8
freeze-dried chicken casserole with peas, soup, pudding	14.7
fresh trout dinner with potatoes, beans, soup, instant apple compote	15.2
freeze-dried pork chops, potatoes, peas and carrots, soup, instant Jell-O	21.3
freeze-dried beef stroganoff, corn, soup, pudding	9.6
3 quart mixes dry milk	18.7
	153.0 or 9 lbs. 9 oz.

Organizing the Food

After you have decided what food you will take, there is a lot you can do at home to make packing and preparing of meals easier on your trip. All unnecessary packaging can be removed, first of all. Coffee, tea, and instant orange juice can be measured for the entire trip and put into separate plastic bags or polyethylene bottles. Dry milk can be bought in bulk and bagged in quart amounts to save money or simply purchased in quart sizes. Liquids, as oil and syrup, can be put into small polyethylene bottles. Certain foods can be made at home and bagged as trail bars, granola, fish breading mix, biscuit and pancake mixes, and hot oatmeal breakfast.

Once all the food for a given meal, say breakfast, is assembled and stripped of unnecessary packaging, it is put into a medium-sized plastic bag, securely tied, and labeled. This bag is then placed with other breakfast bags into a large plastic garbage-sized bag labeled "breakfasts," into which has also gone the coffee, a tub of margarine, the oil, and anything else needed for breakfasts. The same system is used for dinners. For lunches, the food is not freeze-dried with different menus for each day, so all the cheese, salami, dried fruit, and everything needed for lunch is placed in a large bag labeled "lunches." The snack food can be put into the smallest child's pack.

This compartmentalization serves several purposes. First, it helps organize the amount of food needed for the intended number of days on the trail. Second, it helps organize the packs by having the food for each meal separate. Third, the plastic bags help keep out moisture in case of rain, and they make good garbage containers to pack out later. Last, this system facilitates the preparation of any meal. When everything needed is all together, mom and dad's sanity is preserved, and the appetites of the kids are appeased that much quicker. When we arrive at a campsite late in the afternoon, we are usually quite hungry and in no mood to search through all the packs to scrounge up the fish breading mix. Prepacking allows you to open the dinner bag and pull out the menu that sounds good.

Emergency Rations

We believe in being optimists, but there is no excuse for being foolhardy. Therefore we always carry a full day's extra rations in case we are held up by a bad storm, injury, or any other reason. This does not mean an elaborate day's fare, just an extra hot breakfast, a couple of extra soups, and an extra dinner entree. Since all these items require cooking, we are not tempted to eat them up as snacks.

To summarize, a properly chosen freeze-dry diet supplemented with protein-rich foods can satisfy adults and children while backpacking. We once met an older couple while on a ten-day backpacking trip. They lived entirely on freeze-dried foods to cut down the weight of their packs. They admitted they felt progressively weaker as the trip went on. By supplementing the menu we find we do not become weak. We (but not the children) usually lose weight during a long backpacking trip because of all the exercise we get each day. But the weight loss is just the spare tire accumulated over the winter.

It is important to pack along the heavier natural foods to provide quality protein and vitamins for the body which has to be refueled regularly to work well. These foods make for variation in the diet and improve the taste of foods that might otherwise become tiresome.

It has been our experience that we have never suffered any ill effects from the diet described over extended periods of time (two to three months). We have, on the contrary, thrived. It has been heartwarming to see our children brown and sturdy, full of energy, and without coughs or sniffles whenever we are backpacking.

Wild Foods

Sometimes it may be necessary or desirable to supplement the diet. The food may be getting low and you are not ready to go home, or it has been a long time without fresh foods. If a person is *well informed* of the flora and fauna that occur in the locality the family will hike in, certain wild foods can be enjoyed.

For trips in excess of seven days, we have found the twenty-one meals can be stretched out by supplementing our menu with fresh fish at every opportunity. Fishing is probably the easiest and safest way to vary the menu. It is also relatively undamaging to the environment as long as care is taken to bury fish entrails and bones well and to use care not to overtread fragile lake edges. On one extended trip in the Wind River Range, we found that after nine days we still had three complete breakfasts and dinners remaining plus several assorted soups. The trout fishing had been superb, and we could have undoubtedly managed several more days had we not planned a specific exit date. Besides, we were beginning to smell a bit like the local fish market, not to mention our flagging interest in yet another meal of fish.

Fresh greens are always a welcome addition to a dinner. Sourgrass or watercress makes a tasty impromptu salad. Pick the greens while they are young and tender and wash them right in the stream they are growing by. One summer in the Alaska Range we enjoyed refreshing salads nightly while the greens were plentiful. They were, in fact, our only salads that summer with the going price of lettuce eighty cents per head!

If you are in an isolated area (not in a state or national park that prohibits picking of plants or parts of plants) and know

Two edible plants. Left: sourgrass, or mountain sorrel (*Oxyria digyna*), 6″–12″ high, reddish flowers, dark green leaves. Drawing taken from Ann's collection of Alaskan plants. Found along streams in damp places and along rocks. Right: watercress (*Rorippa nasturtium aquaticum*), found floating in cold streams and lakes, forms mats, flowers small, white, and inconspicuous. Drawing adapted from *A Field Guide to Rocky Mountain Wild Flowers*, John J. Craighead, 1963, p. 68.

your berries, a trailside treat is to be had for the picking. The Alaska Range has to be the blueberry capital of the world. Nowhere else have we seen such huge, sweet blueberries in such quantities. They also add to your vitamin C intake, as do strawberries, raspberries, blackberries, and any other edible wild berries. The children love to pick berries, and both became champion pickers (and eaters). Such an activity makes a nice break from the hiking, and it is educational for your children to learn more about the plants around them.

Fly mushroom (*Amanita muscaria*), an example of a poisonous mushroom. Keep children away! This photo was taken in Minnesota. The mushroom is off-white with reddish to yellowish spots on the top. The "petticoat" and "death cup" are characteristic of this species. It is listed variously as "deadly," "poisonous-hallucinogenic," and "poisonous and dangerous but rarely fatal" in different mushroom guides.

Be sure to keep a careful eye on your children when it comes to picking and eating *anything.* It pays to be very strict about this as there are berries, leaves, roots, and entire plants which are poisonous in one way or another. We tell our children never to pick anything before showing it to one of us first. We explain that it is often difficult to tell poisonous plant life from that which is edible, and that it is for their own good that we make this rule.

This rule applies especially to mushrooms which should be left strictly alone unless you are an expert or have taken a course in mycology from an expert. There are so many mushrooms that are fatal to an adult, let alone a child. One bite of the Amanita muscaria can be fatal. We have taken a mycology course but even so dare not venture past the more commonly known puff balls and coprinus types.

We were in a campground in Minnesota once just after a heavy rain. We took a walk through the grounds and found to our dismay an average of half a dozen Amanita muscaria fungi growing happily in almost every campsite! We immediately sought out the ranger who had not realized the danger. He ran and got his shovel.

Mushrooms must be respected, but they can still be enjoyed for their infinite variety of color and form. Just be sure your children do not touch them.

In general we do not like to pick plant life and encourage our children not to—particularly wildflowers growing alongside a trail. We explain that there will be others after us who will want to enjoy their beauty and fragrance, which fade immediately once picked. We have become more and more aware that to disturb even one plant is to detract from the whole scene. Man's duty is increasingly to leave no sign of his presence and to teach his children to do likewise.

Drinking Water

Now that you are packed to the hilt with all kinds of dry food, the problem is to find water. It may not be a problem if you are in an alpine wilderness area in early June. It may be if it is September at a lower elevation. Obviously all the dry food in the world is useless without good water. With children it is imperative that a dependable source of water is known and accessible. In most high mountainous areas where streams are well aerated and draining from unpopulated, and therefore unpolluted, ground, the water should be safe. Beware though of still lakes that do not appear to harbor any kind of life, areas where stock graze, or overused campsites.

We routinely carry two one-quart polyethylene bottles. The wide cap variety are the most convenient for pouring in dry ingredients. They are also easier to drink from. Normally the bottles are never both full en route from one place to

It is important to drink plenty of water when backpacking. This stream beats the kitchen tap at home any day!

another. At least one pint is consumed when we stop for a drink, and the remainder usually lasts until the next stream. One full poly bottle weighs two pounds as opposed to five ounces empty. In country where running water is plentiful, it makes sense to carry the extra one empty.

Mixing instant mixes in a quart poly bottle can be quite a trick. After a little practice, you can pour the contents of the premixed packet into the bottle, and then gingerly touch the open lip of the bottle to the surface of a stream in such a way that the bottle fills about half way up. Then screw on the cap and shake vigorously until the solution is well mixed. Finally, fill the bottle the rest of the way up by the same method. This is a good job for kids, but not if their balance is still uncertain. A full poly bottle sinks quickly, but more importantly, so might your child.

The importance of sufficient fluids cannot be overstressed. We urge the boys to drink their fill on every occasion, although small bladders mean extra stops along the trail. There are lots of ways to insure that everyone has an adequate liquid intake. Premixed drinks of various flavors are good, particularly the lemonade drinks, which seem to be the best thirst quenchers. Both at breakfast and dinner, hot chocolate is satisfying. The individual hot soup packets have been very handy when we were waiting out a storm.

There are occasions when it is necessary to carry extra water, even in mountainous terrain. A glance at your trail route or topographic map will reveal whether you will follow a stream or not. The latter was the case with us on one trip in the Wind River Range. Little did we know that the entire route from Spring Creek Park to Glimpse Lake would be dry. The trail had been changed away from the creek, so we were six miles without being able to replenish our water. It was a gradual uphill climb on a warm August day. Lovely lakes and streams came into view a thousand feet below us, but we were not about to descend and reclimb that distance. Fortunately we had nearly a full quart of lemonade to start, and as it became apparent we would remain on a ridge for the duration we arranged a bit of rationing between us so that the boys would have enough. We also took pains to take the creek trail on the way back. This was a case of not knowing exactly where the trail was going to go because it was not marked on the trail map. We knew where we were because we also had a topographic map. We had anticipated that there would be no major water sources, but we had thought we would find some small creeks or ponds. We learned from this experience that it is a good idea to check with the forest service people about particular trails before setting off on them.

Another example of when you must carry extra water is when you think there is a good chance that you will not make it to the next water source. This happened to us going out of Elkhart Park in the Wind River Range one afternoon. Due to a number of circumstances, rain, car problems, etc., we got a late start and did not even get on the trail until 2:00 in the afternoon. The consensus of the family was that we would go as far as we felt like and carry extra water, which we did. It turned out that we probably could have made the five miles, but we were interrupted by a thunderstorm just as the trail crossed a large open meadow. Being prudent we decided to stop for the night and take shelter in the woods and hopefully have a drier start in the morning. Again the situation called for rationing, but it was not uncomfortable as we had carried fresh foods for that night's dinner which did not require any water for cooking and which were also high in water content (lettuce and a cucumber). The rest of the water was then available for drinking. The only minor inconvenience was that we had to postpone brushing our teeth and doing up the breakfast dishes.

Recipes

As you backpack yourself, you will undoubtedly develop your own recipes as we have done. Here are some combinations that work well for us:

Breakfasts

GRANOLA: *Makes 12–13 cups, enough for 3 breakfasts (4 servings each)*

Mix in a large bowl:
6 cups old-fashioned rolled oats
3 cups wheat germ (raw)
1 cup sesame seeds
1 cup sunflower seeds
1 cup nuts
1 cup coconut, unsweetened (optional)
1 heaping teaspoon salt
1 heaping tablespoon brewer's yeast

Heat in saucepan till warm:
1⅓ cups honey
⅔ cup polyunsaturated oil
1 teaspoon vanilla

Add to above ingredients and mix thoroughly. Put in buttered 9- x 13-inch baking pan. Bake in 300° oven 30 minutes. Stir. Bake 30 minutes more. Remove from oven. Stir. Let cool. Put in airtight container. To serve, just add cold milk and fruit, if desired.

HOT OATMEAL BREAKFAST (*Serves 4*)

Mix in a medium bowl:
3 cups quick-cooking (not instant) rolled oats
½ cup dry milk
½ cup wheat germ (raw)
½ cup raisins
1 teaspoon salt
1 teaspoon cinnamon
¼ cup brown sugar

Store in airtight container. To serve, put in bowls and pour boiling water on top of cereal to moisten to taste.

BISCUIT OR PANCAKE MIX (*makes 8 medium biscuits or pancakes*)

1½ cups unbleached flour
½ cup wheat germ (raw)
1 teaspoon salt
3 teaspoons baking powder

Store in airtight container.
For buckwheat pancakes or biscuits use ½ cup buckwheat flour.

For biscuits:

To above mix add ⅓ cup oil and ⅔ cup milk or enough liquid to make a soft dough. Knead briefly, pat flat, cut out biscuits with cup, place in preheated frypan. Cook slowly until brown on bottom, turn, repeat. The biscuits rise better if you can cover the pan with a metal plate or foil.

For pancakes:

To above mix add ⅓ cup oil and 1¾ cups milk or enough liquid so pancake batter is of consistency that is easy to pour. If you want to get fancy you can also add a package of dry eggs (2). That will make the pancakes rise more.

To save another step in the cooking you can mix the dry milk in with the rest of the mix so you only add water in the morning. We have milk on hand to drink anyway, so for us this is not a problem. Oil in the mix is not really necessary if you oil the pan each time you cook with it. Some people use Teflon pans. In this case the oil just makes the pancakes taste richer and doubly insures against sticking.

Lunches and Snacks

OATMEAL AND SESAME-SEED COOKIES (*Makes 16 1½ inch squares*)

½ cup softened margarine
1 cup packed brown sugar
1 egg
3 tablespoons milk
1¼ cup quick-cooking rolled oats (not instant)
1 cup raisins
1¼ cups unbleached flour
1 heaping tablespoon brewer's yeast
½ teaspoon each salt, baking soda, and cinnamon
1 cup sesame seeds

Cream margarine and sugar till blended. Beat in egg and milk. Stir in seeds, oatmeal, and raisins. Sift dry ingredients into above and mix well. Pack into buttered (margarined) 9 x 9-inch pan. Press down with hand. Bake in 375° oven 12–15 minutes or until browned lightly. Cool. Cut.

TRAIL BARS (*Makes about two dozen 1½-inch squares*)

Melt in saucepan:
1 cube margarine
2 squares chocolate
1⅓ cups honey
1 teaspoon vanilla

Mix in large bowl:
1 cup sesame seeds
1 cup coconut (unsweetened)
1 cup nuts or sunflower seeds
1 cup wheat germ
3 cups rolled oats

Sift into dry ingredients and mix in:
1½ cups unbleached flour
1 teaspoon salt
1 tablespoon brewer's yeast

Mix in melted ingredients until thoroughly blended. Pack into 9 x 13-inch greased pan. Bake in 375° oven 12–15 minutes or until browned. Let cool.

DRY FRUIT PEMMICAN (*Makes about two dozen 3-inch logs.*)

Put through a food grinder:
1 cup dry apples
1 cup dry apricots
1 cup pitted dates
1 cup dried, pitted prunes
1 cup raisins
1 cup sunflower seeds
1 cup coconut

Then mix in ½ cup peanut butter (not hydrogenated), ½ cup melted margarine, ½ cup honey, 1 tablespoon brewer's yeast.

Mix together well, form into rolls. Roll in powdered sugar. Wrap in waxed paper and store in airtight container. Can freeze.

Dinners

FRESH FISH BREADING MIX

1 cup unbleached flour
1 cup raw wheat germ
1 teaspoon salt
1 teaspoon paprika
few shakes ground pepper

Shake up in plastic bag and seal with twist tie.

FREEZE-DRIED BEEF CASSEROLE WITH CARROTS

At home:

Measure 2 cups noodles into plastic bag and seal. Place in dinner bag: noodles, 1 packet gravy mix (beef), 1 packet freeze-dried beef, 1 packet freeze-dried carrots.

In camp:

Measure 3 cups water into large pot. Stir in meat, noodles, and carrots. Bring to a boil. Simmer gently for 10 minutes. During last 5 minutes stir in gravy mix. Serve when all the ingredients are tender.

FREEZE-DRIED CHICKEN CASSEROLE WITH PEAS

At home:

Measure 1 cup instant rice into small plastic bag. Seal. Place in dinner bag: rice, 1 packet freeze-dried chicken, 1 packet freeze-dried peas, 1 packet cream of mushroom soup.

In camp:

Measure 3 cups water into large pot. Stir in rice, chicken, and peas. Bring to a boil and simmer gently for 10 minutes. Add soup mix and stir in. Simmer for 5 minutes more or until all ingredients are tender.

TOPPING (*To put on hot oatmeal, pudding, or applesauce*)

1 cup wheat germ
½ cup brown sugar
½ cup raisins
1 teaspoon cinnamon

Mix and store in plastic bag.

6

Keeping Warm and Dry

CLOTHES FOR BACKPACKING should be comfortable, offer freedom of movement, must be functional. (There is nothing as irritating as pants that bind when you are actively climbing up a steep trail.) When the weather turns inclement, you must have clothes that will keep you warm and dry. You must be prepared for bad weather by having warm and waterproof garments. Maybe you will have perfect weather on your trip, but the chances are much greater that you will experience afternoon thundershowers. At worst you could be enveloped in a regional storm of several days' duration.

We have heard some adult backpackers say that they don't need to take rain gear because if the weather turns foul they can simply hike out. Where young children are concerned, such an attitude is foolish and could be fatal. Young children walk slower and have less interest in endurance hikes. It may be physically impossible for them to make it out in one day, especially if the weather is cold and wet.

Dr. Lathrop has pointed out in his pamphlet "Hypothermia, Killer of the Unprepared" [1] that people have died from

[1] Revised edition, 1972, p. 1.

hypothermia, or the excessive heat loss from the body's core, at low elevations and with temperatures well above freezing. They were unprepared for a sudden drop in temperature accompanied by rain or snow and wind. In several cases, the victims had no extra warm clothing, no tent, little emergency rations, and were tired physically when they started out. If any one of these variables had been reversed, the victims' chances of survival would have been greater.

Therefore in choosing clothing for a family backpacking trip, you want to take clothes for the variety of weather you may experience. At the same time you want to take as little clothing as possible so as not to weigh yourselves down hopelessly. This gets challenging when you have to carry equipment and clothing for more than one child. Everyone has to be kept warm and dry; yet you are not about to pack four suitcases full of clothes!

The basic idea is that while one set of clothes is on another set is off, and in addition you have a warm jacket, hat, and rain gear. We usually wear shorts and shortsleeved shirts to hike in. The second set of clothes is a pair of full length jeans and a longsleeved shirt, for cooler weather. We manage quite nicely with just the two sets of clothes even on trips of ten days or more. If one set becomes too grimy it can be washed and dried out on a nice day.

There are two major exceptions to the two sets of clothing system. The first is if you are to be backpacking in a notoriously wet area, such as Alaska, the Pacific Northwest, or British Columbia. Then you really need three sets of clothes; it only takes two days of rain to soak the first two through. The second exception is if you are toting an infant in diapers who is still crawling. As any parent knows, even three sets of clothes changes for a child in this category is not enough.

In order to have clothing for your children that is both comfortable and functional for extended periods of hiking, it stands to reason it will have to be as good quality as your own. We find down warmer than Dacron, so we made down jackets for our children because at the time we could not find any on the market in small enough sizes. Similarly, we cannot imagine hiking any distance at all in sneakers. Our children should not have to either. We checked out all the shoe places in town plus some mail-order catalogs to come up with suitable boots for them. It is not fair to expect cooperation from small children if they are improperly dressed for the situation. If they are cold or have sore feet they are not going to enjoy backpacking. If their clothes are of the same quality as yours they will enjoy backpacking as much as you do.

The Layer Principle

Mountain weather is very unpredictable. Even weather in the upper Midwest with no large mountains can change suddenly. What the day looks like at 9:00 A.M. is not necessarily an indication of what it will be like at 4:00 P.M. Clothes have to be taken for both hot weather and (often sudden) cool weather. Ideally your longsleeved shirt should fit over the shortsleeved one so that layers of clothing and air work at keeping the body warm.

This layering does not work well with pants. Long pants over shorts will fit too tightly and chafe. The layering is only done with the top half of the body. If you have shorts on and it gets cold, it is best to simply change into long pants and add another layer on top. We have found that we are warm if the small of the back is warm.

How many layers to take depends on where you are going. In wet, cool areas you will need a turtleneck shirt, a longsleeved shirt, a wool or down sweater, a windbreaker, and coated nylon rain gear. In addition, you should have a wool hat and a complete set of long clothes in case the first set becomes wet. Shorts and shortsleeved shirts may not be used at all and should probably be left at home.

In warm, dry areas you will probably wear shorts and a shortsleeved shirt most of the time. You should have in your pack a complete set of long clothes, a down or wool sweater, a wool hat, and a water-repellent windbreaker just in case you do get a surprise shower. Otherwise, the windbreaker will be used mostly for warmth in the evening.

These guidelines refer to areas below 14,000 feet during the summer months. Winter mountaineering and high altitude climbing do not fit into the scope of this book.

The clothing combination you come up with has to be comfortable. If a child's jacket barely fits over a shortsleeved shirt, it is obviously not going to do the layering job. If a child's boot fits just right with a thin cotton sock, try a larger size with the thick wool sock you intend for him to wear when hiking. Knit shirts are more comfortable than fabrics that do not stretch. Well-broken-in jeans do not chafe like new ones. The only way you will know if a given combination will work is to try on all the layers you intend your children to wear in bad weather and see if they can still move around comfortably. If they look and act like mummies, you will have to try something else!

What Kind of Jacket Is Best?

A down jacket may not be necessary for your child. Again it depends on the temperatures where you are going, how cold your child tends to get, how nervous you are about your child getting cold, etc. Thick wool sweaters have been keeping people warm for a long time. Wool is the only material that continues to keep you warm when it gets wet. With a sweater plus a windbreaker, a jacket may not be needed. If you are camping in the Texas hill country you may find a Dacron jacket too warm. It has been our experience that down jackets make the whole family comfortable and happy in a variety of temperatures from 50° F. on down. Of course, the higher the elevation you hike to, the cooler it will get at night.

Hoods

You should have a hood. If your jacket or sweater doesn't have one, your windbreaker or rain gear should. A hood pre-

Down shirts or parkas provide dry, absorbent comfort over a wide range of temperatures. Greg and Chris wear theirs almost every evening when backpacking in the mountains.

vents cold air from getting in around the ears and neck. In very cold weather accompanied by high winds and rain, a hood can make a big difference as to whether one is warm or not. For maximum warmth, the hood should be large enough to accommodate a wool hat underneath it.

When to Switch Layers

Many children will tell you if they are warm enough or if they want their jacket on. But some children, like ours, get so absorbed in what they are doing that they forget to put on extra clothing until they are really quite cold and uncomfortable. If left to supervise their own clothing, they would not enjoy backpacking, for once they get really cold, it takes a long time to warm up, and all the fun is gone from the activity.

You as parents, therefore, have to think ahead a little and anticipate the comfort needs of your child. If we feel chilly we pull out *all* the long shirts. If we feel warm we pack them all up again.

It is important not to get overheated, for that is a fast way to get chilled. As soon as you stop exercising you notice the evaporation of perspiration from your skin, especially when a cool breeze comes along. If the breezes continue while you are still damp you can get quite cold as your body heat gets carried away with the wind.

Therefore try not to let your child get too hot when there is a risk of sudden chilling. There is no problem on a hot day in the middle of the afternoon. But when the sun is about to set, or clouds threaten, it is best not to be perspiring freely. Try to anticipate when it might get chilly, and get out your child's jacket when it clouds over, when the wind comes up, or it's getting late in the day. In mountainous and desert areas the temperature can drop 40° F. or more when the sun sets.

Pajamas

Pajamas, for those who like to wear them, can be a handy extra garment to carry along. Many children are used to sleeping in pajamas. They help keep a child warm in his sleep if he wiggles out of his sleeping bag. They can also serve as long underwear if the weather suddenly gets cold.

Clothes for Babies

For younger babies the one-piece stretch suits are great for backpacking. They keep baby covered up and protected from biting insects, sun, wind, and drafts. As most are synthetic blends, they wash and dry very quickly, enabling you to always have a clean one ready. They also serve as pajamas. Our babies lived in them morning, noon, and night.

When our boys were toddlers we found sweat shirts to be very useful garments, especially the ones that open down the front. Being cotton, they cover up without being too hot or itchy. At night they are useful over pajamas for extra warmth, as our children never seemed to stay in a sleeping bag but crept out during their sleep.

Where to Get Clothing for Kids

Children's clothing can be bought in department stores or sporting goods stores, ordered from catalogs, borrowed from friends, or made by you. We should not forget to mention the garage sale. We found several used boys' turtleneck sweaters, shirts, and pants in one woman's garage, all in good condition and selling for only twenty-five cents apiece!

Jackets

When we were planning a major backpacking trip to the Wind River Range in the spring of 1972, we looked hard for down jackets for the boys but could not find any in stores or catalogs except for the Eddie Bauer catalog which offered a down jacket for $30.00 with no hood. We decided to make them jackets out of ripstop nylon and down that we ordered from Recreational Equipment, Inc. The pattern was McCall's #2998, which unfortunately only goes up to a child's size six. Thus it had to be altered for size in order to fit our older boy. We also put in gripper snaps instead of a zipper opening; we lengthened the jacket and eliminated the drawstring at the bottom; knit cuffs were attached to the sleeves instead of an elastic casing; the jacket inside and outside pieces were cut identically and sewn together to eliminate facings. And of course we used down between the layers instead of quilted material. (See the illustrations for more details.) We figured it cost about $16.00 to make. As of 1975 this parka would cost almost $20.00 to make.

Since that time several companies have added children's down jackets to their catalogs. Eddie Bauer now offers a hooded down jacket for around $40.00. Eastern Mountain Sports' catalog has a hooded down parka with a coated nylon shell for slightly over $40.00. They also offer a 60/40 down jacket with a shell hood in the $30.00 range. Powderhorn Mountaineering has down jackets for children by special order.

For those who don't want to spend as much money for a ready-made parka and yet don't feel like tackling a down parka from scratch, a good compromise is to use the increasingly popular kits. They are reasonably priced and come with full instructions. Frostline includes down jacket kits for around $20.00, depending on the size of the child. Down hood kits come separately at about $4.00 or $5.00. Holubar

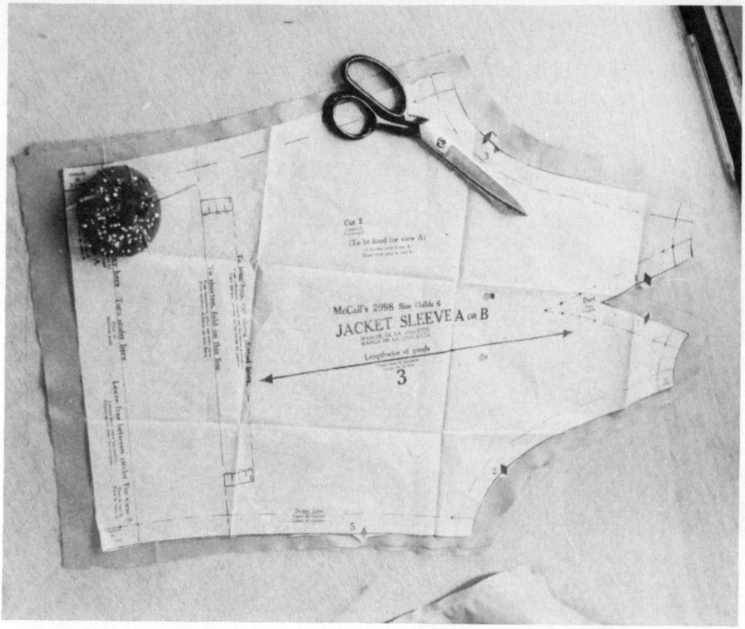

Steps to parka-making: Lay out pattern. Alter if necessary. Here sleeve is enlarged. Cut twice as many pieces as pattern says. Thus there are two "outsides" of every piece. Pieces are stitched right sides together on machine except along one edge. Turn piece right side out.

offers a down jacket kit for about $20.00 with the hood kit coming extra, running from about $5.00 or $7.00, depending on size. They also have a child's down sweater kit with less down for under $15.00 and a mountain parka kit for about $17.00. Sun Down, a new company in southern Minnesota, is also offering kits that include clothing for children. Their child's down vest kit costs from $8.00 to $12.00 depending on size, and their down jacket kit without hood costs from $12.00 to $17.00 depending on size. They have recently added a 60/40 mountain parka for kids and a down hood. Check the catalog for latest prices.

We have not discussed windbreakers for children because, although they are very nice, we had to draw the line some-

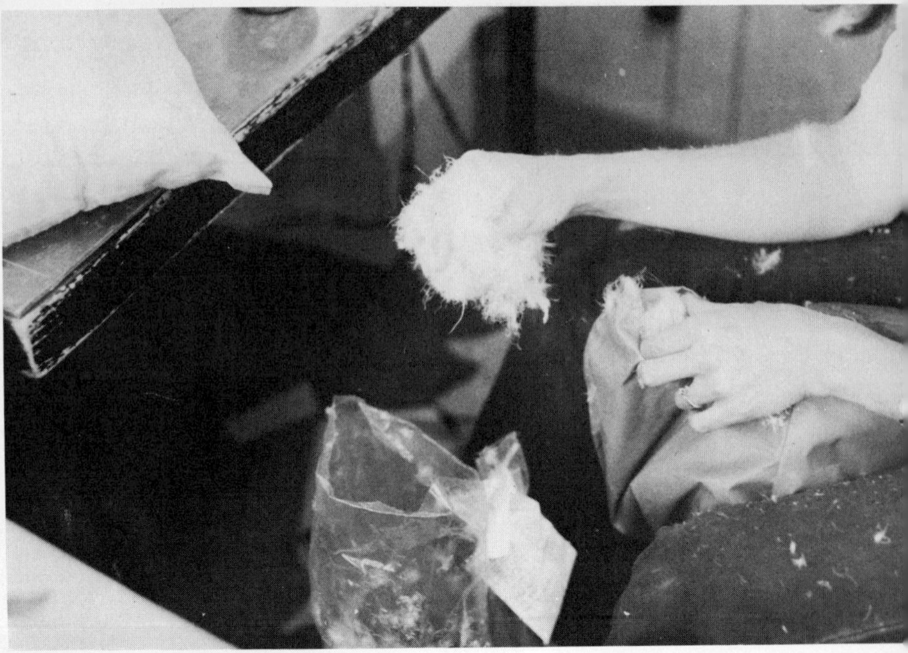

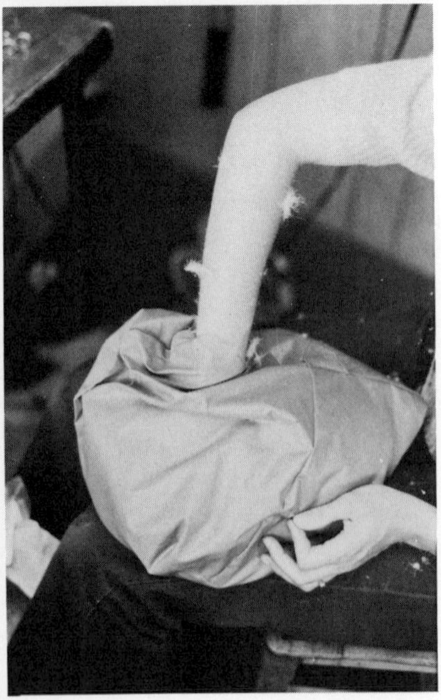

Stuffing: The down is carefully grabbed in the plastic bag and quickly transferred to the piece and pushed into the bottom. Down will automatically rise. The trick is to get the down into the corners.

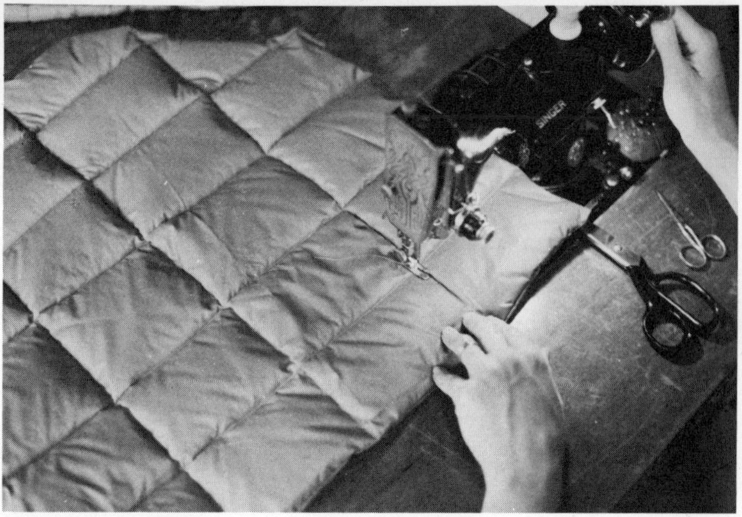

When each piece has been stuffed, tuck open raw edges to inside and topstitch opening closed. Then it is ready to quilt. To quilt, stitch through all thicknesses, making even divisions.

Finishing each piece: Here the sleeve has been sewn together and the cuff attached. It is now ready to attach to the body of the parka. When all the pieces are finished, sew them all together, attach gripper snaps to front, and run drawstring through hood.

where on weight, so our family carries rain gear that is truly waterproof rather than windbreakers. We personally have not backpacked with the children in wet, cool areas where we would have had to carry both windbreakers and rain gear. When the children can carry more of their own clothing and equipment we will take on some wetter areas, such as the Olympics in Washington where you can expect rain any time.

Rain Gear

Children's yellow rubberized slickers do not breathe well and are much heavier than the newer garments made out of coated nylon. We prefer the long, hooded, coated nylon raincoats. Ponchos, in our experience, are too floppy in wind to keep one dry, and rain pants get one too wet from perspiration to be comfortable. This is our personal choice. For the benefit of those who like ponchos, some sources for those will be included.

In the ready-made category, Eastern Mountain Sports has a child's rain parka for about $12.00 with pants for slightly over $10.00. Both are made of coated nylon. Kreeger and Son has a child's poncho also. (All are around $10.00.)

Frostline has a poncho kit for $6.00, rain pants for about $4.00 and rain parkas for $6.00 to $8.00. All are made of coated nylon. Holubar also offers a child's poncho kit for about $7.00. Sun Down has a poncho kit for about $6.00.

Boots

Suitable hiking boots are most important for a successful backpacking trip. Tennis shoes are just not sturdy enough. Because the soles are made of rubber they do not breathe,

Leather boots for children provide ankle support, good breathability, and firm footing. They have psychological benefits too, because they are "just like" adult boots.

and feet get too hot and sweaty. Because they are low cut they let in trail dust, making the feet terribly grimy and uncomfortable. Most importantly, tennis shoes do not support the ankles well enough during climbing and descending, leading to sore, tired feet, and wobbly, perhaps turned ankles.

Several good boots are on the market for children, and not all of them are expensive. Kinney's and Penney's market an excellent child's boot with genuine Montagna Vibram soles for around $12.00 to $16.00 depending on size. Sears and Ward's market a boot with higher arches and a hard, rubber sole, which we have found tends to slip on rock. It has been our experience that Vibram soles have better gripping qualities. Soft lug soles are also good.

Some catalogs offer good choices in children's boots, but they are more expensive. Recreational Equipment, Inc., has three different boots with lug soles ranging in price from about $18.00 to $23.00. Eastern Mountain Sports offers two child-sized hiking boots. One costs about $18.00, and the other costs slightly over $20.00.

Whatever the choice, it is imperative that the boots be well broken in before any serious hiking is attempted. This means several day trips over varying terrain are in order. It is also a good idea to treat new boots with a protective coating. This will make the boots water repellent and help them last longer. Sno Seal is excellent. Silicone sprays are also available.

Socks

Most ordinary department stores or children's shops are hopeless when it comes to wool or wool-blend socks for children that are nice and thick. Sporting goods stores are improving, and discount stores, Ward's, and surplus stores are finally carrying this type of sock in small sizes. We would not think of hiking in thin, cotton socks all day. Feet need the absorption and comfort of a thick sock. Wool is best as it stays warm when damp.

Be sure to take along the thick socks when you have your child try on hiking boots. He may take a whole size larger with the thicker sock on.

Guarding Against Too Much Sun

So far we have been talking about how to keep warm and dry when the weather is inclement. We also have to protect ourselves from too much sun. Sunburn, dizziness, even sunstroke can result if one goes unprepared. Two important things to have are a hat and sunglasses.

Sailor caps, with the rim turned down, are our favorite hats for the boys. Their ears and eyes are protected from excessive sun, and the hat offers some protection from insects. This type of hat is heavy enough so that it does not blow off in the first breeze that comes along. The first time we went backpacking with the boys was when they were almost four and two. It was impossible to get them to wear any kind of conventional lightweight sun hat. Finally we tried a straw cowboy hat with a drawstring under the chin. It proved to be a most difficult hat! The drawstring irritated their necks. The slightest breeze sent the hats wafting away. Furthermore when they were not being used, they did not stuff gracefully into a pack, but demoniacally popped out again. The straw would break off, getting into the food. Sailor type hats can be found in any department store.

Sunglasses may seem superfluous for small children but they are good insurance against general eye strain and snowblindness when crossing snow fields at high elevations.

It is important to get truly polarized sunglasses as the nonpolarized glass does not block out the potentially dangerous ultraviolet light rays. This is most important at high elevations where there is more glare from light-colored surfaces, reflection from water or snow, and where the air is thinner and therefore absorbs less radiation.

To check if a pair of glasses is polarized, rotate the glasses 90° and see if the view becomes darker due to the light being absorbed. If they are not polarized there will be no change. Most drugstores offer children's polarized sunglasses.

If the glasses seem to fall off the child easily, you can attach a large rubber band or piece of elastic to the earpieces and adjust it so that it feels comfortable to the child. This way he will have a hard time losing them.

How to Cope with Diapers

It might seem impossible to backpack if your child is still in diapers. This is not so. We successfully backpacked with our child who was not yet two who wore diapers day and night, and with the same child the next summer when he still wore diapers at night.

First of all forget about throwaway diapers. Why? There is no garbage can! You are the can, and this fact must be remembered always if we are to keep our wilderness beautiful. It is impossible to burn a soaked paper diaper. In the hottest of fires they are belligerently nonburnable. They are not easy to bury—there is too much paper for squirrels to dig up later, and plastic is not biodegradable. But you don't want to have to pack out untold pounds of soggy, shredding, smelly lumps of paper. Moreover, enough fresh paper diapers for a trip take up too much space in the pack to be practical. It may be possible to lay out the wet diaper in the sun and reuse it if your child is not subject to diaper rash, but with this kind of treatment he will probably develop it!

We have found it much easier to carry regular diapers and wash them out. A dozen non-prefolded diapers are sufficient for a trip of any length providing you wash out the diapers every other day and there is an hour of full sunshine to dry them out and sterilize them. Even without sunshine a good wind will dry diapers out in no time. The volume of one dozen diapers can be very small if each diaper is rolled and stuffed into corners of the clothing section of your pack. We also find diapers make dandy towels in a pinch. As they are lightweight, this may be what your youngest would like to carry in his pack.

Clothes Washing

The washing of clothes is a necessary part of backpacking, especially with young children. They somehow get filthier than they do at home, which really doesn't matter except that if it is wet dirt, there is a danger of chill. No one likes being cold, and part of the purpose of washing clothes is to insure that there is always a spare set of clothes, dry and comfortable for any contingency. It is a fact that clean clothes are warmer than dirty ones, for air is a better insulator than dirt. On a cold day, it is nice to have clean, warm clothes to put on. The fastest way to discourage children from backpacking is to let them get wet and cold with no spare clothes. You have to arrange things so this does not happen, as they do not have the foresight or the ability to do so themselves.

This brings to mind a day one summer when we found a campsite along a major trail skirting a large lake. One problem with popular trails is that the obvious campsites begin to resemble overtrodden, dusty national park campsites. The natural cover of pineneedles and small plants at this site had been walked over so many times that it ceased to grow, exposing the dirt underneath. We had hoped to press on to a better spot, but the children were tired of hiking, so we stopped there anyway. In short order both children were covered with dust, playing car with small sticks, pushing them through a couple of inches of beautifully ground dirt. Then they helped us fish, and the dust became mud. The kids didn't mind being muddy—they were having a ball—but we winced at the thought of their muddy bodies in their down sleeping bags. In five minutes warm water was ready, the boys were stripped (the sun was still up) and washed and put into their clean pajamas and sleeping bags for the night. Then their clothes were rinsed out and hung on trees to dry overnight. As it was fair weather, the clothes were dry by morning.

The easiest time to do a washing is right after a meal as the

Drying diapers on tree limbs or pack.

stove is set up and going. A pot can be heating up while the dishes are being washed. Under no circumstances should clothes be washed in the water source. Even final rinsing will get out soap scum and dirt, which will contaminate the drinking water.

We use a collapsible plastic bucket to haul water several yards away from the water source to a place where the soap will not run right back in. Add a panful of hot water, a small squeeze of biodegradable soap, and you are in business. It pays to use very little soap. The more you use the more water you must haul to rinse it all out. Cold water is fine for the rinsing. It takes too much fuel to heat the rinse water.

Once the clothes are washed and rinsed you can survey the

terrain to find something to hang them on. Trees make dandy drying racks, especially pines. Boulders are good too, if you can find clean rocks to anchor the clothes. Or you can hang the clothes on your tent if it has an exterior frame or ropes. Of course, if you carry extra cord in your pack you could rig up a temporary clothesline. If there is no time for clotheslines, you can tuck the edges of the clothes in your pack pockets and proceed to hike on the trail. Unless it is raining or excessively dry and dusty, the clothes should be dry and fresh-smelling in a couple of hours.

There is no need to be dirty while backpacking. It just takes a little effort to fit clotheswashing into the routine. An added boon is how clean your hands get in the process—a real plus after a couple of days on the trail!

Summary

Take what you need but no more. A swimsuit, for example, is really superfluous in the backcountry. Underwear can serve modest folks; skinny-dipping is fun!

It may be helpful to review an actual day to see how the clothing works out. One summer day in the Big Horn Mountains we woke up to brilliant sunshine. We all put on shorts. The boys did not even bother with their shirts, it was so hot. We decided to take a day hike over a nearby ridge to explore the country off the trail and to do some fishing for the fabled golden trout in the more distant lakes. We took the smaller pack, filled it with clothes, lunch, camera, and fishing rods, and were off. About 11:00 some clouds drifted by, occasionally covering up the sun. Everyone put on shirts. By 11:30, the sun was staying under, and a wind had come up. On went the longsleeved shirts. We continued to hike over the ridge and down the other side to a large stream where we had lunch. The clouds appeared to be gathering for a storm—perhaps by late afternoon. We got out the down jackets and put on our long pants. After enough fish had been caught for dinner and we had started for camp (it was about 3:00) it started to sprinkle. Out came the rain gear. It started to rain in earnest. We took shelter in a grove of spruce trees. When the rain subsided to a mere drizzle we again started for camp. By the time we arrived (around 5:00) we could take off both rainclothes and jackets as the sun came out for a brief period while we were fixing dinner. By 6:00 the clouds were back and the jackets again went on.

We had used all our clothes, and we had stayed warm and dry, which is the important point.

Basic Clothing List for an Average Backpacking Trip

On everyone:

- underwear
- shortsleeved shirt, shorts
- wool or wool blend socks, hiking boots
- hat

In pack, accessible:

- longsleeved shirt
- long pants
- down jacket or heavy wool sweater
- rain gear with hood, or water-repellent, sturdy windbreaker with hood
- wool hat
- extra set of underwear
- 2 extra pairs of wool socks
- sunglasses
- pajamas, if used

List of Suppliers for Children's Clothes

Down jackets, ready-made:

Eastern Mountain Sports
1041 Commonwealth Avenue
Boston, Massachusetts 02215

Eddie Bauer
P.O. Box 3700
Seattle, Washington 98124

Powderhorn Mountaineering
"The Tetons"
P.O. Box 1228
Jackson Hole, Wyoming 83001

Down jacket kits:

Frostline Kits
Department C
P.O. Box 589
Broomfield, Colorado 80020

Holubar (Carikit Outdoor Equipment Kits)
P.O. Box 7
Boulder, Colorado 80302

Gerry, Div. of Outdoor Sports, Inc.
5450 North Valley Hwy.
Denver, Colorado 80216

Sundown Kits
P.O. Box 1023
Burnsville, Minnesota 55337

60/40 mountain parka:

Holubar (see above for address)

Rain gear, ready-made:

Eastern Mountain Sports (see above for address)

Kreeger and Son
30 West 46th St.
New York, New York 10036

Rain gear kits:

Frostline, Holubar, Sundown (see above for addresses)

Boots:

Eastern Mountain Sports (see above for address)

Recreational Equipment, Inc.
1525 11th Avenue
Seattle, Washington 98122

7
On the Trail

Last Minute Checks

Once you have reached the trailhead by car or other means, you may want to rest from the traveling, get organized, and make last minute checks on equipment and food supplies. Do you have enough white gas? Matches? Food? Does everyone have their rain gear and an extra set of clothes? At this stage a checklist is useful. (See diagram on page 128.) The checking is also done at home before departure, of course, but since we use our equipment en route to our kicking-off point, we always have to reorganize somewhat when we arrive.

There is enough to do to get ready that we usually take the remainder of the day instead of being in a hurry to get on the trail immediately. Our children are always tired after car travel and like time to themselves when we arrive at our destination. This is a good time for them to explore the campsite, help set up the tent, or simply play by themselves. This interlude also gives them a chance to become familiar with the area and to get used to the idea of the backpacking trip before actually setting off. By the next morning, everyone will be refreshed and ready to start.

Loading the Packs

Loading the packs should not be difficult if things have been organized at home. It is still a good idea to doublecheck the meal bags to see if they are complete and if there is an extra day's ration along in case of emergency.

What goes where will depend on the construction of your pack. Some packs are divided into two or more compartments, and some have only one central cavity. We have one of each, and the way we organize their contents is shown in the diagram. All of the children's clothes fit into the bottom compartment of Ann's pack where they are easily accessible without disrupting the contents of the top compartment. If an infant is along, the bottom compartment can contain diapers, baby powder, extra baby clothes, and a strong plastic bag for dirty diapers. In the top compartment of Ann's pack go both her bag and Chris's in the same stuff sack. The lunch bag goes on top of that with Ann's and Chris's rain gear to top it off. This way everything that is needed for the day is handy. If it starts to rain you don't want to have everything get wet while you dig out the raingear. Three foam pads, rolled up tightly, are attached with cord to the frame of the pack under the rest.

In Jim's pack, which has just one large compartment, we place the tent and tent fly in a vertical position next to Jim and Greg's down bags stuffed into the same sack. On top of the bags are the Svea stove and cook kit followed by the breakfast and dinner bags. None of these items will be needed until the end of a day, normally, and thus should go at the bottom of the pack. Next in line are adult clothes in separate stuff sacks, followed by Jim's and Greg's rain gear. Jim's pad goes right at the top.

Jim's pack

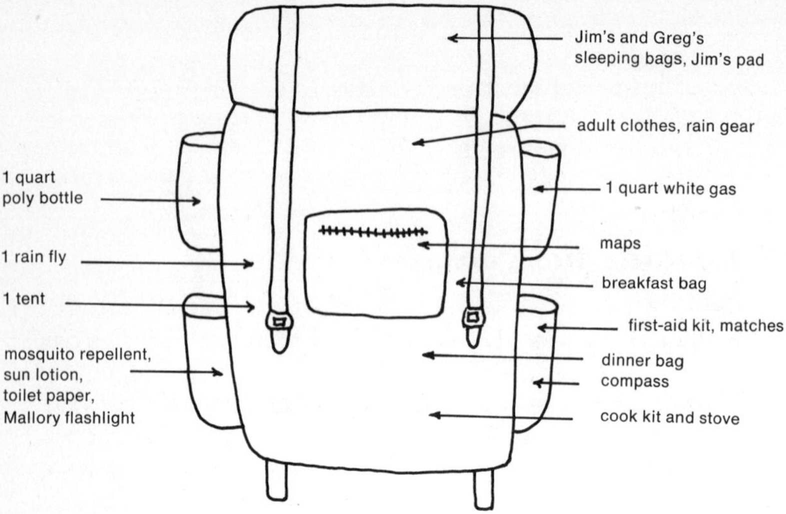

Ann's pack

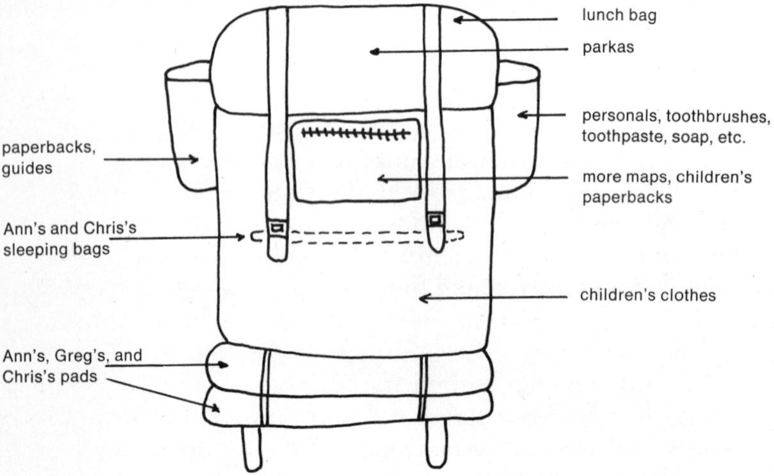

This is how we organize our packs. Loading the packs is a good opportunity to teach children why the rain gear and lunch go on top and why the first-aid kit is in a side pocket.

The side pockets of both packs are very useful for those little things you want handy like the first-aid kit, suntan lotion, paperbacks and nature guides, lip balm, topographic maps, mosquito repellent, matches, sunglasses, and toilet paper. Our packs have deep side pockets that are large enough to hold quart-sized poly bottles. This makes thirst-quenching easy and quick. If you are toting a small child a side pocket can be devoted to his needs—trailside snacks, as bits of cheese or apple, crackers or teething biscuits, an extra diaper, pacifier, or bottle.

Children pick up the logic of organization quite readily and can be encouraged to provide suggestions. For example, ask them what they would need most if it were suddenly to rain. Ask them in the morning where the lunch sack ought to be and where the snacks and candies should be when they stop for a trail break. Not only does this become a learning process but the children become an integral part of the operation and thus are more interested and enthusiastic. They would certainly like to pack their own packs.

In the children's packs go small, lightweight, but important items. For example, at the age of two and one-half years, Chris carried his hat, sunglasses, and some lemon drops. The lemon drops were very important in his mind, and as a result he rarely forgot his pack after a trail break. At the age of four and one-half, Greg carried his down jacket, hat, and sunglasses. The important thing to remember is to keep everything they carry light so they will not get discouraged at this early age. As they get older they can carry more of their own things.

This arrangement is one that has worked well for us, and should not be considered the only way or the best way to organize a pack. Packs vary widely in size, number of compartments, and in the size and number of exterior pockets. Perhaps the best guide to individual organization is to anticipate what your needs and their sequence are likely to be during the course of a normal day and pack accordingly.

Registration

Before you actually get on the trail, it is important to register your plans with the resident forest ranger or supervisor. At most major trailheads in national forests and parks are sign-in books in which you should indicate names, number of people in your party, destination, and duration of your trip. In many regions, however, these registrations may not be checked frequently, and thus they serve little purpose in case of an emergency. A better procedure is to check in directly with the local ranger, tell him your plans and the fact that small children are included. We always report the maximum number of days we plan to be away and say that we will check back on our return.

This is also a good time to ask about the condition of the trails you plan to use. The ranger will be in contact with the trail crews and can forewarn you about hazardous stream crossings, poorly marked trails, and other aspects of your trip that could not be anticipated. He will also know if any bears have been sighted or if domestic animals are grazing in the area, which would mean not drinking from certain water sources. Sometimes you can get updated maps that may not have been ready when you wrote earlier.

Taking It Easy

When packs are finally hoisted up and you take the first steps on the trail, remember: Take it easy. Everyone in the family or group must start out with a good attitude or problems will spring up right away. On one of our trips, we had spent the morning on last minute organization and exploring around the trailhead. We were anxious to get started so that we could cover a couple of miles before lunch. Just as we got

Be sure to register before starting a trip in the backcountry. Tell the local forest ranger or supervisor where you are going and when you plan to return.

our packs on and adjusted, Chris suddenly developed a passionate interest in a gravel pile near the parking area. When he displayed a genuine reluctance to leave immediately, we simply took our packs off and waited. In a few minutes, Chris was ready to go, and we all departed in a good frame of mind.

Once on the trail, remember that your adult goals and expectations may require modification at any moment. We always plan ahead for likely lunch sites and, of course, suitable campsites in the afternoon. But if trailside diversions en route consume more time than anticipated, a change in plans may be in order as an alternative to rushing children along. In our experience, small children will enjoy the backpacking adventure if they are not pushed or nagged or repeatedly told to hurry up. A trip like this will work only if both parents are not in a hurry and react positively to what the child can and undoubtedly will find interesting along the way.

Keep in mind also that children's goals are usually very simple. Heading for a stream crossing because there may be tadpoles there, or aiming for a lake because we can go wading there, are goals a child can understand. His enthusiasm for the idea is enhanced if he can see what he's aiming for. A small child won't be much interested in a lake that's a mile away. If he does not see the lake, it does not exist for him, and he won't be motivated to get there. Nor can a small child appreciate a lake simply for its scenic beauty. A lake is interesting to him when he knows what he can do there. When he gets there he can fish, swim, make a cold drink, or play on the beach. If you help your children to anticipate what is coming up and enjoy with them the many spots of interest along the way, they will look forward to each new trail as an adventure.

Progress on the Trail

Obviously a balance must be achieved between the interests of your children and your own goals. If the trip becomes totally unstructured and no progress is made at all on the trail, then your primary objective is defeated. That is, they will not realize the satisfaction of traveling on their own power through the wilderness. If reasonable progress is lacking, there are several things you can try.

Take it easy on the trail. If someone lags behind because of something more interesting than walking on the trail, relax and enjoy the scenery.

We normally discourage running on the trail, but in open places like this it can do wonders to motivate progress in the desired direction.

Children who balk on the trail are usually not tired but tired of *walking*, so try changing the pace. Have the kids skip or hop or run. Suggest a race. Their packs aren't heavy. It is a real contest when your three-year-old challenges you with your loaded pack. If you have two children they may enjoy racing each other. We give our youngest a head start to make a fair race. Be sure to check the trail ahead for possible obstructions. Small ones are easily tripped up by logs, rocks, and uneven terrain when they are running. A well-worn, wide trail is ideal for races. A meadow is even better. The boys always get across them before we do. It sometimes helps to take their packs so they can run unhindered.

Although we do not normally encourage running on the trail, races like these provide a momentary pick-up which often leads to other games. Sometimes we have chugged along happily for a whole mile imagining ourselves as trains, jets, racing cars, or whatever the favorite means of locomotion is at the moment. On steep grades, we sometimes recount the familiar children's story of the little train that could. "I think I can, I think I can" and finally "I know I can" has gotten us over more than one steep section of a trail.

Then there are more serious activities along the trail that require some responsibility. This appeals to children. For example, going first on the trail means being leader of the group. And the leader of course must be able to follow the trail. This is a simple task on well-worn trails, but a good trail often degenerates to rocky surfaces marked only by an occasional cairn. This is one of the best times to teach children about finding their way. When the trail begins to degenerate, have the leader stop and look carefully ahead. Encourage him not to proceed until a trail marker is spotted. It may be a rocky cairn, a slashed tree trunk, or brightly colored tape, but have him spot it by himself. In less traveled regions, the trail often disappears in broad meadows. Or in heavily traveled areas, a meadow may have too many paths. Which trail to take? The clue is often found by simply looking across the meadow in the direction you are traveling for a gap in the trees. Or you may spot the trail where the ground is higher. Looking well ahead for better marked segments of a trail is particularly useful in high alpine areas where mixed rocky and meadow terrain is common. Kids are very quick to pick up these concepts, once they know what to look for.

Another factor that stimulates interest in being first on the trail is the prospect of seeing animals. If this is an objective, encourage your children to lead quietly, and again, to look well ahead on the trail. Most wild animals will dart out of sight as soon as you come into their view. If you have your eyes focused only a few feet away, you will miss a lot.

Occasionally the responsibility of being last on the trail has appealed to Greg and Chris. We try to teach them that we can go no faster than the slowest person in the group. The last person sees to it that no one falls behind, or that nothing falls out of a pack. When Chris was in diapers and we looped freshly washed ones over packs while we walked, Greg occasionally walked behind to insure that nothing would be left on the trail. Another responsibility of being last is announcing when another group is coming up faster from behind. In the case of pack trains, it is best to move well off the trail to let them pass. If you have the family dog along, it is important to restrain your pet so that he does not upset the horses or get kicked by them.

When the going gets slow, another effective way to get little minds off the act of walking is conversation. We were once absolutely amazed at how talkative Chris suddenly became on the first backpacking trip of the season. Holding Jim's hand as we hiked along, Chris talked about anything and everything. We theorized that after the long winter months during which the boys were in school and Jim worked at the office, Chris was simply enjoying his father's undivided attention for a change. And his father was having a fine time, too. Chris covered an incredible range of subjects from the most serious to the most absurd. The subject of gravity and how the earth orbits the sun is pretty heavy trail conversation for a two-and-a-half-year-old. Chris had apparently picked up parts of our adult discussion on the long drive from Minneapolis. On the other hand, we got off onto some delightful quizzes about food. "What do you think my favorite dessert is?" queried Jim. The boys guessed and guessed, and the miles seemed to roll by. As interest started to wane, Jim professed that his favorite dessert was an onion milkshake! If Greg and Chris's laughter was any indication, that had to be the funniest comment ever echoed on that remote mountain trail. The boys still go into hysterics whenever the subject comes up.

Interest in moving on the trail is enhanced when we set an observable, short-ranged objective for a rest stop. For an example, designate the next switchback or the stream at the bottom of the hill as a formal stop where packs are taken off, everyone has a drink, and perhaps a trail snack. Do not be too ambitious in setting the goal. Distances are deceptive, and the common tendency is to underestimate mileage from one point to another.

Rest stops are a good time to check feet for the first signs of blisters. Occasionally progress on the trail is slowed by a slight discomfort that has not developed to the stage where a bona fide complaint is in order. A slightly tender area on an ankle or toe where a sock was doubled over can lead to a full-fledged blister in a hurry. And kids are notorious for ignoring slight discomforts (like a full bladder) if they are engrossed in some activity. So at regular intervals we ask the boys how their feet feel. If it is a hot day, everyone will enjoy taking boots and socks off, and especially swishing their feet around in a cold stream or lake. See to it that socks are on straight and even before you set off again.

If all ideas fail, you may then conclude that your children are, in fact, physically tired. This certainly happens, and you must take care that you do not overextend your children. If they are bone-tired, you should stop for the day. Here is where the flexibility of backpacking really pays off.

Except for water requirements, backpackers are completely self-sufficient. At any time a camp can be set up. Usually by midafternoon you can tell how things are stacking up. If junior is having an off-day you can plan on stocking up at the next stream so that you can settle into the first campable site that comes along. Day hikers have to make it back to the car. Backpackers don't, so don't worry about the master plan. As long as you have water you can set up practically anywhere.

On the other hand your child may only be tired temporarily. Time and again we have noticed unusual bursts of energy after we stopped for lunch. Just the change is refreshing. Anyone gets tired of doing something too long. Dragging behind is also common about 3:00 in the afternoon. A rest and a snack, and our boys are usually ready to go. The same thing happens around 5:00, and then they get a new pick-me-up after dinner. One time, after a very long day, both boys decided to climb a nearby rocky ridge after dinner. It was nearly one hundred feet high. They ran up and down it twice just for fun! They also found the energy to zoom back and forth from the lake we were camped by. While backpacking it is often the parents who are carrying the load who tire first. Kids are resilient. After a meal and a brief rest, they are raring to go.

In short, we have found that if we don't rush and if we give the children plenty of time to play on rest stops, they move along the trail fairly well. The main thing that seems to hold children up on the trail is apparently not fatigue but greater interest in doing something other than putting one foot in front of the other.

Trail Etiquette

In the process of having fun and games on the trail, keep in mind that other hikers may be rudely made aware of your presence. We discourage loud yelling and unnecessary noise. Children must learn that acceptable behavior on the trail (and in camp) means not disrupting the quiet and solitude that someone else may be enjoying. Greg and Chris seem to respect this, but they are equally impressed with the fact that loud noises will scare animals and birds away. We try to teach them that we are in the natural home of wild creatures, and that we should disturb them as little as possible.

When Greg and Chris are leading on the trail, we encourage them to proceed independently, but we are careful not to let them get too far ahead. When another group approaches, either from ahead or from the rear, we move off the trail and let them pass. This is a good habit to get into for safety reasons. In many areas, especially in our experience on the east side of California's Sierra Nevada, professional packers will release their pack animals high in the mountains permitting them to return untended to base camp. On two occasions we have encountered pack horses barreling down a narrow trail. This is dangerous, and potential encounters of this sort should be avoided. As a matter of policy, we try to avoid the large trails used by professional outfitters.

Another aspect of trail etiquette we believe in strongly is not littering. Few things disturb us more than finding gum and candy wrappers and other litter left thoughtlessly on the trail. We believe keeping trails clear of litter is the personal responsibility of each individual hiker and is therefore a responsibility that our children should learn. One exterior pocket of Greg's pack is devoted to small bits of aluminum foil, paper, orange peels, and other miscellany we find on the trail. Of course it is not our primary objective to clean up after other people, but every little effort helps, and we often make a game of it. The boys try to spot all litter on the trail, and the adults try to spot the litter they miss. As a result of emphasizing this point, neither boy would dream of dropping their own litter on the trail. It is gratifying to watch them automatically stuff a cellophane wrapper into their pocket as they are going along. It gives us hope that they are learning to care for their environment.

We as adults are so addicted to this ethic that knowing a piece of trash is around can momentarily spoil our wilderness experience. An experience illustrating this happened to us near Landmark Gap Lake in the Amphitheater Mountains in central Alaska. We were just finishing a five-day trip into a remote region where probably no more than a dozen people per year pass through. It was raining, and we were tired. Suddenly on the trail ahead was an empty beer can. Judging from its rust, it had spent the winter there. Dutifully the can was collected as well as four others in plain sight along the trail. As these items usually come in sixes, we looked for another can but didn't spot it, down the hill beneath an alder, until we had passed by. The impulse was to leave it. As we walked on, we rationalized that the lone can would probably never be seen again by passing hunters or fishermen, and even if it were, no one would particularly care. Two hundred yards down the trail Jim couldn't stand it any longer. He took off his pack and went back to fetch that sixth can.

This is what we mean by personal responsibility, and it is the kind of behavior we hope to instill by example in our children. It takes so little effort to leave the wilderness unspoiled, and the rewards of doing so are immeasurable.

Another subject deserving of special comment is the matter of trail preservation. Children as well as adults must learn to stick to the designated trails even though taking shortcuts is fun and saves distance. The switchbacks are there for a good reason, for without them, the route up would be no fun. At the start of a five-day trip from Onion Valley on the east side of the Sierras we were met by a troop of boy scouts storming down the mountainside. After the dust settled we started up the trail. The damage was obvious, even to Greg who was only three and one-half years old at the time. Every switchback had been short-circuited, leaving a chute of gravel, rocks, and dust. Two disrupted waterbars reminded us that more damage would be done by erosion when the overdue rains came.

The boys were too young then to be left with any lasting impression. On many occasions since then, however, we have made a point of showing them how switchbacks and waterbars are placed to preserve trails. Now *they* point out to *us* where other people have cut switchbacks.

What to See

We always encourage our children to learn about the plant and animal life along the trail. Whether you are on a major backpacking trip or just strolling through a neighborhood park, nature is just brimming with interesting and rewarding discoveries. The biggest problem is teaching children (and adults) *how* to see. Once this is mastered, *what* to see comes almost automatically. To learn how, you must take some time. A hurried trip will miss nature's more subtle offerings every time. You must stop and pass an hour or so just looking around at the grass, shrubs, and trees. All sorts of things will suddenly appear that went unnoticed and hence unappreciated on busier occasions.

We have passed many pleasant hours in high alpine meadows just looking. We once stopped for a drink from a small, grass-lined brook that meanders lazily through a meadow near Wyoming's Cloud Peak in the Bighorn Mountains. We had a fleeting glimpse of a white-tipped fin as we approached. The stream was no more than eighteen inches wide and seemed much too small to support trout. It never attracted fishermen. We departed but then very quietly returned a few minutes later. We took care to step softly so as not to disturb the trout we suspected was there in the tiny brook. Sure enough, after a few minutes of patient waiting, a handsome brook trout resumed his feeding along the grassy bank in clear view of all.

This meadow had yet more to offer. We departed from the trail at this point to explore further along the brook. We immediately encountered small, doglike tracks along a sandy bar. Four toe and claw marks on each track were enough evidence for the boys to conclude that a fox had been there and that he had been traveling upstream. A little later on we found some larger tracks, but this time there were only two "toes" instead of four. These were the characteristic split-hoof tracks of mule deer, and judging by the splayed hoof marks and the distance between them, it looked as if the deer had been startled and had run from the meadow.

The same little meadow was full of holes of various sizes. Most of them were homes for squirrels, but one large hole looked big enough for our fox friend or even a badger. We spent several minutes speculating on the kinds of creatures that might live there.

After our meadow adventures, we proceeded further on the main trail. We were suddenly stopped in our tracks by a

A friendly marmot looks us over from his perch high in the rocks. He blends in so well that only his movement and his whistle betray his presence.

piercing whistle. None of us saw the creature, but we knew he was somewhere in the rocks above the trail. We all remained still until the whistle came again. We looked intently toward the rocks but still couldn't see him. Then Greg whispered, "I see him." He pointed to a slab of gray granite on which the marmot was perched, his brown coat and white collar blending perfectly with his surroundings. When asked how he spotted it, Greg replied that he saw the marmot move his head a little bit. Otherwise he would have probably remained undetected. Thus, Greg learned that motion is easy to spot, and that is the reason why many animals remain quite still until you are almost upon them.

We have observed this time and again, and each time the boys understand a bit more. Ruffed grouse in the western states are notorious for exploding into the air right before your feet. That happened to us once near treeline north of Fremont Lake in Wyoming. It nearly scared the wits out of us. We had almost stepped on the bird before it took flight.

Over the five summers we have been backpacking with our children, we have had encounters with many different wild animals, including bears, sheep, moose, and caribou in Alaska, and nearly all of the commonly observed wild mammals in the western states. Each encounter was pleasant and without dire consequences, simply because we have always respected the rights of the animal to be in his environment. As visitors, our objective is only to observe.

Greg and Chris have readily accepted this concept. On one trip in Wyoming's Wind River Range, we had been out on the trail for six days, and were en route from Elbow Lake near Gannett Peak to Upper Jean Lakes (see Chapter 9); two men appeared on horseback and both had hand guns, strapped around their hips. We passed the usual pleasantries, and they went on their way. Greg and Chris stared dumbfounded, and then were silent for minutes afterward. Finally Greg asked the inevitable question, "Dad, why did those men have guns?" That was not an easy one to answer. We gave the optimistic opinion that those men probably did not understand the wilderness, and felt they needed protection from wild animals. The thought seemed absurd in this high alpine country with the peaceful marmots basking in the sun.

Aside from the animals, there are countless other discoveries waiting if you take the time to look. We enjoy searching out and photographing the many wildflowers that abound in all wilderness regions. The boys have learned many of the common ones by name, especially those with interesting names like elephant's head, monkshood, shooting star, bluebells, and buttercups. If you are interested in wildflowers, a paperback guide is handy to have along and well worth the few extra ounces.

We discourage the boys from picking wildflowers along the trail. Each one they pick is one less for the next person to enjoy. If we are off the beaten track, however, and there is a great abundance of a particular variety, then it does no harm to pick a few. Chris learned a lesson quite on his own one spring day. He had picked a handful of beautiful lupines and was admiring what a lovely bouquet they made. He hung on to his bouquet for another half hour as we hiked along the trail. When we came to a rest stop, we asked Chris how his flowers were. He replied, "They are not very pretty now," showing us his wilted handful of once lovely lupines.

On all of our trips, we like to make a game of finding as many different flowers as we can. We keep a notebook and photographic record of each new discovery. Our record is 103 different kinds during a summer in the Alaska Range. The boys delight in this activity. It is common to find a dozen or more different kinds in a single meadow. With a little experience, you learn which varieties are sun lovers and which are shade lovers, or which prefer open rocky ground, and which prefer marshes.

The different kinds of trees you are likely to encounter provide a learning experience, too. The boys can readily identify birches by their white, papery bark and spruces by their tall, symmetric form. We once stopped for lunch in a lovely stand of birches, and we got on the subject of birch bark canoes.

The boys were fascinated to learn that Indians at one time actually constructed canoes from this natural material.

Another tree the boys are familiar with is the Jeffrey Pine. They encountered their first one high in the Sierra Nevadas, and thought it was just another pine tree. But upon detecting the delectable vanilla fragrance of the bark, they have not missed a Jeffrey Pine since. On more than one occasion passersby on the trail have looked on quizzically as Greg and Chris proceeded systematically to sniff the trunks of every tree in sight.

The children learned early that the inner bark of certain trees is food for porcupines. We have seen the scarred trunks of trees on numerous occasions where hungry porcupines had been at work. Once in Wyoming's Medicine Bow mountains, we found the same scars, but this time they were six feet off the ground. There was little doubt that a rodent was responsible. The incisor marks were clearly visible. "But how big do porcupines get?" asked Greg. We asked him what he thought these mountains looked like in the middle of winter. He concluded that it would be cold with lots of snow. He then smiled, realizing that porcupines eat in the wintertime too, and they have to walk on top of the snow. Later that day, we estimated winter snow depths by the porcupine damage.

Then there is the fascinating world of insects. Chris delights in overturning rocks to discover beetles, ants, sowbugs, centipedes, and other small, many-legged creatures. Observing such discoveries with a magnifying glass is additionally fascinating. Jim always carries a ten-power hand lens no larger than a thimble that he uses to examine rocks and minerals. When focused on a tiny insect, an incredible new world opens up. Greg was so captivated once with the behavior of a mosquito on his arm that he allowed it to probe and even withdraw blood before deciding he had seen enough. Caterpillars, inchworms, moths, butterflies—all are transformed in an impressive manner under a hand lens.

Binoculars are fun, too, if you don't mind carrying them. They are great for watching and identifying birds. Some need no binoculars to see, of course, such as the bold jays, who try to steal your lunch, or the dramatic mama ptarmigan who tries to lead you away from her babies by putting on a great show of lameness.

Binoculars are also good for viewing shy wildlife, such as mountain sheep and goats, that usually never come anywhere near humans. In Wyoming once we had not seen any wildlife in the area when we went to bed (except for the trout in the lake), but when we awakened, there was a young bull moose having his breakfast of water weeds at the swampy end of the lake. The wind was in our favor, so that he didn't pick up our scent for about twenty minutes. The boys had a good look at him through the binoculars while he grazed.

When we go on backpacking trips we try to teach our chil-

A Canada jay, or "camp robber," joins us for lunch. He blended into his environment so well the boys did not spot him at first.

dren something of the interdependence of plant and animal life. At this age, they have heard us talk about ecology, and they know the word refers to the relationships between all living things and their environment. Some aspects of this complex relationship they have seen for themselves. Hopefully as they grow older they will see much more. Ultimately, we hope they will understand how man, too, should fit into nature's balance—not as a conqueror, but as an integral part.

Hazards to Watch Out For

There are always hazards in the outdoors, but in general they are few and of less consequence than ones you would normally find in the city. The major difference is simply one of familiarity. In the city, you teach your children at an early age to look both ways before crossing a street. After a while they automatically are alert to the danger. In the outdoors, it is the unfamiliarity that makes hazards seem ominous. The solution is to know the hazards—how to recognize them, and how to avoid them. In the following pages we have listed many hazards that might be met on the trail. Recognition of these and others not included here is largely a matter of exercising common sense.

Stream Crossings

Special attention must be given to stream and river crossings when children are involved. Even the smallest streams require the guiding hand of an adult because of wet and slippery rocks. In some cases, it is easiest to simply straddle the stream or part of it and hoist the child through the air from one side to the other. Most mountain streams have fast, narrow stretches that are tempting to jump, and wide, shallow stretches that can be easily and safely waded. We prefer the latter option because it offers the least chance for an accident involving the children. Besides, shallow streams are fun to wade.

A heavy rainstorm can quickly turn an easy stream crossing into a raging torrent that would turn back even the boldest adults. Such was the case when we crossed the middle fork of the San Joaquin River near Devil's Postpile in California. One morning, we crossed safely using several large logs laid across a shallow, slow-moving part of the river. We had enjoyed several days of hot, dry weather, and the water was quite low. But then it rained hard for a day and a night. The following morning, the placid little river had seemingly increased its speed and volume tenfold. By the looks of small trees in the current and the sound of boulders bouncing along the bottom, there was little question that an adult could easily drown if a crossing had been attempted in that part of the river.

Snowbanks

In most mountainous regions, snowbanks remain well into July and August. If you plan a backpacking trip at high elevations anywhere in the western states during the month of June, you can count on sections of trails being covered with snow. These present potentially hazardous situations. Footing is always difficult for children because their legs are not long enough to reach from one adult boot hole in the snow to another. As a consequence, they must walk on top of the snow which may be icy or, at the very least, slippery.

On level surfaces this is not much of a problem. But as the season progresses, snowbanks linger on the protected sides of slopes and in small valleys. Trails that traverse the surface of a steep snowbank are particularly dangerous because a slip there will usually not end until the child or adult slides to the bottom of the bank. In the spring snowbanks of this sort can extend for several hundred feet, and are often so crusty

Snowbanks surrounded by rocks are potentially hazardous situations. In tough spots it is best to hold hands.

that once you have fallen and start to slide downslope, it is virtually impossible to stop without an ice axe. Any adult who has gone through this experience will attest to how quickly you accelerate and how terrifying the rocks at the bottom appear.

On hot summer days, the upper few inches of snowbanks exposed to the sun soften up and make for safe travel. Such snowbanks can be deceptive, however. On a warm August day in the Wind River Range we crossed Lester Pass at an elevation of over 11,000 feet. We had made the ascent from Seneca Lake on a northwest facing slope free of snow. On the back side of the pass, we were confronted with a mammoth snowbank that must have been a windswept cornice the previous winter. The well-worn trail disappeared beneath the soft snow; because of extensive melting the trail was obliterated. As the snow was ideal for boot-skiing, there at first seemed little problem descending the snowbank. But then the surface suddenly became extremely hard and crusty where the slope steepened near the bottom. This was caused by freezing of meltwater during the night. Fortunately, we recognized the hazard and were able to choose an alternative route. In case of doubt, it is always best to have an experienced adult break the trail first to insure a safe route. On several occasions, we have found it necessary to go completely around a dangerous snowbank even though it meant going a half-mile or so out of our way.

The other potentially hazardous situation with snowbanks is where they cover streams. It is very common to hear a gushing stream beneath large snowbanks. As summer progresses, the snow melts and eventually caves into the water. At the transition point, a slip on the snow can mean an ice cold dousing. Children have a strange fascination with running water, and are easily tempted to walk across soft snow to see a rushing stream. The edges of the snowbank near the water are the thinnest of all. Even the weight of a thirty-pound child is enough to break through.

Our rule of thumb for snowbanks is to hold hands. This gives the child the handle he needs to navigate the slippery surface, and it insures that in the event of a fall, he will not go out of your reach.

Precipitous Trails

Our rule for particularly steep trails is the same as for snowbanks and stream crossings: We hold hands. Even on the best maintained trails, you are likely to encounter sections where the trail is narrow and bounded on one side by a precipitous slope, cliff, or river. Take the children in hand until you have passed by the spot. Under no circumstances should children be permitted to run on such trails. Some children have a real fear of looking down several hundred feet from a rocky brink and are reluctant to go near the edge. Other children don't have this fear and don't hesitate to go right up to the edge. Chris is definitely in the latter category, so we have to physically restrain him. We don't want to instill an unreasonable fear of falling in him, but we do want him to learn that loose rock and soil around cliff edges can cause a fall.

Brushy Trails

Nearly every mountain trail will have sections, particularly at lower elevations, where alders and other low-lying vegetation grow over the trail. When the family is hiking along, it is easy to forget that the waist-high alder that an adult would brush by is a face-level hazard for a small child. In order to avoid accidents from the snapback of trailside vegetation, have everyone space out on the trail. This is good trail policy in general. No one appreciates another's company right on his heels.

Weather

It is important to keep an eye on the sky. Weather conditions can change very quickly, especially in the mountains, and you do not want to be caught unprepared. In regions above timberline, not only can you get thoroughly soaked in just a few minutes but there is always the danger of lightning. If a storm is coming do not stay on an exposed ridge where lightning may strike. Head down for the lower lands where there are plenty of trees. An isolated tree on an open plateau could attract lightning. Another reason for heading for the trees is so you can take cover from heavy rain, wind, and even hailstones, which can get pretty large in severe thunderstorms. Seeking shelter in the forest also gives you a temporary home in the event a big storm has hit and layover plans are in order.

In our experience, hiking in a downpour with children has never been fun. Everyone eventually gets wet, if not from the rain coming down, from the puddles in the trail, wet bushes and grass, or just from condensed perspiration beneath waterproof rain gear. Footing becomes precarious, especially where slippery rocks and fallen trees must be crossed. In short, it is just easier and safer to wait out a storm, overnight if necessary. If the storm looks temporary, you can stay remarkably dry beneath a dense grove of firs. The accumulated needles are almost always dry and make a comfortable couch. The branches overhead serve as a sort of thatched roof. On numerous occasions we have set up our little stove in such a spot and had a hot cup of soup or a whole meal to pass the time. If there are no trees, and you are too far above timberline to retreat, set up the tent in a low place, if possible on the downwind side of the storm behind some rocks to break the wind.

In certain situations, it may be necessary to risk getting wet for the sake of avoiding a potentially greater hazard. This is the fall snowstorm that can come to mountainous regions al-

The afternoon storm in the background is about to descend on us. This is no time to play on the trail. Ann carries Chris's pack as he runs for cover.

most anytime after August. Such was the case on a nine-day trip we took to the Cloud Peak Primitive Area in Wyoming's Bighorn Mountains. It was late August. The first six days were beautiful, but the nights grew progressively colder. Our route led us over Florence Pass and eventually to Middle Cloud Peak Lake, approximately fifteen miles from the trail-head and at an elevation of 10,500 feet. The last three miles were off the main trail and above timberline. At dawn of our seventh day there were three inches of heavy wet snow on the ground and more on the way. With three days of food and an emergency ration remaining, we made the decision to proceed out as originally planned rather than wait the storm out. The prospect of hiking in the wet snow was not appealing, because everyone was sure to end up with wet, cold feet. Yet the possibility that the storm would last another two or three days and drop a foot or two of snow presented a potentially worse situation. Without a trail, the three-mile stretch over broken rock and talus would be extremely hazardous with additional snow. Three hours later we were all warm and dry again in our tent near the main trail. From there, we knew we could proceed safely and rapidly even if it continued to snow. Fortunately, the storm passed that night and we encountered no further difficulties.

Getting Lost

In going off the trail to find cover from a storm, don't go too far lest you become confused and lose your way back to the trail. Pick out specific landmarks as you go and turn around frequently to see what they look like from the way you will be returning. It helps to follow your route along with a map and mark where you are when you stop. It is also a good idea to check your direction with a compass and then key your location with a map at regular intervals. By using both a compass and a map (topographic ones are more accurate) you should know where you are at all times even if you are not on a trail. Compasses are fascinating to children who love to see which way the arrow will go. Don't be concerned if the mileages shown on the trail maps don't agree with the trail signs. They are usually estimated and may vary slightly.

If you are new to backcountry travel, map and compass reading, it might be safer to stick to the well-marked trails that have signs with mileages posted at regular intervals. Then as you get used to maps you can venture farther from the trails.

In little traveled regions, it is common for trails to disintegrate into several smaller trails and eventually into no trail at all. This often happens in the spring when travelers break new trails around extensive areas of snow. When the snow melts, there is some uncertainty as to the correct way to go. Equally common is the situation where you come upon an unmarked fork in the trail. In each of these situations, a little trail savvy is all you need to find the correct route. This means knowing exactly where you are on a map at all times and knowing the direction you should be going to arrive at your destination.

The most important thing to remember if you happen to lose the trail is not to get separated. It is foolhardy to split up the group with the idea that the trail will be more quickly found. That can end with each person not only lost but alone.

However, we have successfully found the correct fork of a trail at an ambiguous intersection by sending one adult to scout out the trail while the other stays with the children. Usually a secondary trail disintegrates or gets obviously overgrown with plant life after just a few hundred yards. Or the trail you are scouting may take a turn in the opposite direction you want to go. Then you can scout out the other trail to see if it is better or if a sign comes up.

Needless to say you should always keep track of your children, and if they are very small, they should always be in sight. Some families insist that all children be equipped with police-type whistles. These can be tied on a string around each child's neck. The ground rule is that it should never be blown unless he is lost or in need of help, or unless it is in reply to an adult whistle. We have not used whistles simply because our children do not tend to wander off. Each child is different. As parents, you will know your children and their wandering tendencies.

Overexposure

Excess exposure to the sun at high elevations can have painful consequences, particularly to children. The rarified air at high altitude combined with high heat reflectivity from light-colored rocks and snow result in sunburn and chapped lips far more quickly than in other situations. Small children and infants have sensitive skin and are more prone to overexposure than most adults.

The way to avoid this hazard is to insist that hats and sunglasses be worn. (See Chapter 6.) Combine that with liberal usage of suntan lotion and lip balm and you have the problem largely prevented.

On the first day out on a backpacking trip there is a temptation to strip to the waist in order to soak up the sun. If everyone has pale skin from a long winter indoors, this is reckless. It is best to break in slowly, starting with a shortsleeved shirt and shorts for the morning and then changing to longer clothes in the afternoon.

Poisonous Spiders

Fatal bites from spiders are extremely rare. In fact, fatalities from wasp and bee stings due to individual allergic reactions are more numerous by far than those from spiders. It is still a good idea to know the poisonous spiders in order to avoid them.[1] Children are especially prone to bites as they

[1] Herbert W. and Lorna R. Levi, *Spiders and Their Kin* (New York: Golden Press, 1968), p. 16.

are closer to the ground, slower moving, and more curious than many adults.

The female black widow (the male doesn't bite) is shiny black with red on the underside of her abdomen. She likes dark places like the insides of mailboxes or among damp, dark rocks. Her bite will cause severe abdominal pain. Black widows occur in most warm parts of the world.

The brown recluse is our other poisonous spider, occurring in the southern parts of the United States. It is brown, has a violin-shaped mark on its body, and is somewhat fuzzy, unlike the smooth black widow. Its bite will cause a nasty wound and has been known to cause deaths in children. Spiders, however, don't go out of their way to find you. If someone is bitten by a nonpoisonous spider, wash the area and apply a clean dressing as for any wound. (First aid for a poisonous spider bite will be discussed at the end of this section.)

The species of tarantulas found in the United States are not considered to be poisonous, and are sometimes kept as pets. However, the hairs on their legs can be quite irritating to human skin. They are found in the Southwest. So if you are in dry areas watch out for them. A bite from a nonpoisonous tarantula just requires washing and a clean dressing.

Likewise, scorpions are to be avoided for their painful sting produced by the stinger at the tip of their tail. The most dangerous species found in the United States is in Arizona. Species in Mexico have caused deaths. They occur throughout the West and South in cool, damp places, not in the hot sun.

Poisonous Snakes

There are five poisonous snakes in the United States. There are two kinds of colorful but highly poisonous coral snakes. Both have alternating red, yellow, and black bands. They occur in the Southwest and Southeastern United States. The copperhead occurs in the uplands of the Southeast. It has beige and brown hourglass markings. The cottonmouth occurs throughout the South in swampy areas. It is large, thick, and has dark brown markings. The massasauga and pigmy rattlers occur in the Mid- to Southeastern United States in wetlands and uplands, respectively. Larger than these, thirteen other species of rattlesnakes occur throughout the country except for the upper Midwest and Northeast.

It is rare that a poisonous snake will attack you. These creatures are usually willing to leave you alone—unless they are molested or surprised. Ask the forest ranger in advance if snakes are prevalent, and if they are watch where you put your hands and feet. Don't climb around carelessly on dry, sunny, rocky ledges where you might surprise a snake. We have seen very few snakes in all the years we have been backpacking and never at elevations above 8,000 feet.

First Aid for Bites and Stings from Poisonous Snakes, Spiders, Scorpions, and Bees

Fortunately, none of our family has ever been bitten or stung by such creatures. Therefore, we cannot speak with firsthand authority on how to administer first-aid treatment. Small children are particularly susceptible because of their curiosity and lack of experience. A child's smaller body volume and his greater vulnerability to neck or head wounds make immediate first-aid treatment necessary.

There appears to be some controversy over the most effective first-aid treatment for snakebites. There is the traditional method of applying a tourniquet, cutting into the wound, and using suction to remove the venom. This is described in all standard first-aid texts. The improper use of the tourniquet, the cutting of blood vessels, tendons, and nerves; and the possibility of subsequent infection are some of the disadvantages.[2] Moreover, the shock and mental anguish of the treat-

[2] Dennis Bleything, *Primitive Medical Aid in the Wilderness* (Life Support Technology, Inc., 1971), pp. 21–24.

ment itself could have additional bad effects for a small child.

An alternative first-aid treatment that is gaining popularity in snake country is the application of cold packs, ice, or snow to the bite. Cold stream or lake water is also effective. The purpose of applying cold is to retard the progress of the venom until medical aid is reached. There are instant cold compresses available in drugstores that are inexpensive and weigh only a few ounces. One we are familiar with is manufactured by Kwik Kold (Cutter Laboratories). A chemical reaction that absorbs heat is activated inside a plastic package that is applied to the affected area. Care must be taken not to freeze the wounded part, and the victim should be kept warm and quiet. Avoid the use of painkillers and alcohol taken internally.

The appropriate treatment, particularly where small children are involved, will depend on the situation. Medical attention should be sought in any event. If you will be traveling in arid areas where snakes are common, ask your doctor what specific treatment he recommends in view of each person's previous medical history.

Bites and stings from poisonous spiders, scorpions, and bees are generally less serious than from poisonous snakes. Because the amount of toxin is minute from these smaller creatures, the traditional "cut-and-suck" technique is impractical. Application of cold packs is effective and helps reduce the pain associated with the bite or sting. Again, a doctor or other authority should be consulted beforehand in case any member of the family has special allergies to bee stings and the like.

Ticks

When hiking through brush country be alert for ticks that tumble off plants onto you. They attach themselves with their mouthparts and suck the blood of the host. In both the East and West of the United States they can transmit Rocky Mountain spotted fever. Mostly they are annoying but not dangerous. We check each other frequently to make sure we have not picked any up. Take particular care to check scalps as ticks like to burrow underneath hair. Often by frequent checking you can catch them before they attach themselves to you.

If a tick does manage to latch onto you, you could hold up a match or the hot match head to it (without burning the host, of course) to encourage its retreat. A better method is to cover the whole tick with either oil or alcohol, which suffocates it and forces it to come out. There are many other techniques for removing ticks. Some people use insect repellent to cover the tick. The point is, if the tick has attached himself to you, you don't want to pull him out because that might leave the head in there which could fester. Of course, if the tick is just crawling around looking for a good place to dive in, get it off right away. One reason we prefer high alpine areas is the lack of such annoying creatures, which tend to be found at lower elevations and in dense underbrush.

Other Insects

It is all the other insects which you most likely will encounter—mosquitoes, gnats, flies of various types, ants, and bees, or wasps. All will either bite or sting, but fortunately none are considered poisonous except to a few people who have reactions to them. (See section on first aid for poisonous bites.) If in doubt check with your doctor for medicine to take should you develop a bad reaction. Otherwise use preventative measures like wearing longsleeved and longlegged clothing, long socks, a hat, and lots of repellent. Carry a tent with fine mosquito netting. Shake out the tent and sleeping bags before you settle down for the night, and check around the tent after you are settled in with a flashlight to make sure nothing is lying in ambush for you.

Swelling from mosquito or bee bites can be relieved by the application of cold compresses or cold mud followed by a first-aid cream, if you carry one in your first-aid kit.

There isn't really very much you can do about insects if there happen to be a lot of them around. Check your children often to see that their shirts are tucked in, and that their socks haven't rolled down their ankles. Mosquitoes and black flies, in particular, seem to love to get in between layers of clothing. Keep moving, or if it is the end of the day and there is plenty of wood, a fire that is smoky can be of some help. As a last resort there is always the tent!

Wild Animals

Wild animals rarely present a hazard unless provoked or surprised by man. There is only a remote possibility of a direct encounter with bears or other large animals in a true wilderness area. In their natural habitat, bears want nothing to do with man and will go well out of their way to avoid him. Bears have poor eyesight but incredibly sensitive noses. On several occasions in the Alaska Range we have spotted grizzly bears over a mile away running directly away from us. This has even happened on days when hardly a breeze was blowing.

However, the semitamed bears in Yellowstone Park and other public places have lost their fear of man. The local campground bear looks forward to your arrival knowing that free goodies will be his for the taking. This bear poses a far greater danger than any you would be likely to see in the wilderness. Under no condition should a bear be approached or any attempt made to feed it.

If you should spot a bear on the trail before it gets wind of you, and an encounter seems probable, see to it that your presence becomes known to him. Loud talking, arm waving, and being in a position upwind of it are all effective. This is normally all that is required to avoid a confrontation. If these tactics fail, the only reasonable recourse is to retreat or make a detour. Females with cubs are potentially the most dangerous and should not be taken lightly. The protective instincts of mothers, whether human or beast, can lead to unpredictable behavior. Even a mother ptarmigan can become surprisingly ferocious when her brood is endangered.

If you are concerned about bears, check with the local forest ranger or supervisor. He should know if bears have been seen in the region. Other precautions you should take are to keep a clean camp, avoid cooking bacon and other greasy, aromatic foods in bear country, and avoid storing fresh food in your tent. All food should be stored outside your tent, preferably in a pack hung from a tree limb. This keeps your grub out of reach of bears, as well as porcupines, skunks, and raccoons.

Likely as not you will have pleasant experiences viewing wild animals in their forest homes. One summer in the Alaska Range we made the acquaintance of a beaver family. We hiked by their pond on the way to our camp each time we came back from a shopping trip with packfuls of supplies. It got so they would put on a little show for us by making dives and spectacular splashes with their tails.

Leaving Smaller Animals Alone

Children often want to feed small animals like squirrels and chipmunks. We discourage this for two reasons. Wild animals are used to their own food and may get sick from strange, human food. Also, wild animals are not used to being approached by people and are likely to scratch or bite if they feel threatened.

Skunks, more than squirrels and chipmunks, should be avoided. Not only do they have a noxious spray when provoked, as everyone knows, but they are more susceptible to rabies than smaller animals.

If by chance someone in your party gets bitten by an animal that acts strangely and you suspect is rabid, clean and dress the wound and try to capture the animal. Then pack out and seek medical attention. Most cities have laboratories where they can keep the animal under observation to see if it indeed has rabies. If rabies is diagnosed, then appropriate medical procedures must be followed.

Porcupines do not throw their quills. The quills come out if something comes in contact with them, and because they have barbs on the end they are very painful to remove. They do *not* shoot out as often believed.

Poisonous Plants

Nothing is more irritating than breaking out in a rash from poison oak, poison ivy, or nettles. Young children are not necessarily immune, as some people assume. If you are in any wild area at all, know what these plants look like so that you can spot them before your children get into them. If you do find any of these pesky plants, take the time to teach your children what they look like, if they are old enough to understand. If they are not, you will just have to watch them like a hawk to make sure they don't get into them. This is another reason we prefer high elevations in the mountains—these plants are found lower down.

Poison oak and ivy are woody perennials with dark, glossy, green leaflets in threes. They thrive in both open and shady areas. The ivy leaves are pointed while the oak leaves are more lobed. Even the stems of these deciduous plants exude the oil which causes the irritation. You can also get a rash from handling animals that have been into poison ivy or oak. Above all, never burn these plants. The smoke is highly poisonous.

Washing after exposure immediately with strong soap can minimize the area the rash will cover. For people who are particularly sensitive to these plants, there are shots and oral drops that can be taken prior to exposure that greatly lessen the reaction.

Poison sumac is probably not that dangerous for hikers as it prefers wet areas in bogs, in marshes, and along ditches. Watch for it if you are in this type of terrain. Nonpoisonous

Poisonous plants. Be on the alert for these so that you can show your children what they look like before they get into them. It could ruin a trip. From upper left reading clockwise: poison ivy, poison oak, nettles, poison sumac. Poison ivy and oak can be 6″–12″ high or in large bushes. They can even occur in vines. Nettles are 12″–24″ high. Poison sumac is a shrub 6′–20′ tall. Drawings adapted from *Poisonous Plants in the Wilderness,* Dennis Bleything and Ron Dawson, 1971, pp. 57, 59, 60, 61.

sumacs grow in drier areas; the poisonous variety grows to be a large shrub or tree.[3] The leaves are opposite in groups of ten or more. Often there are greenish or whitish berries hanging in clusters. Nonpoisonous sumacs have red berries.

Nettles are irritating but not poisonous in the sense that they produce only a temporary itching rash that goes away in about a half an hour. The stems are covered with fine barbs that brush against your skin, producing the irritation. They grow in shade or sun.

The worst time for getting poison oak or ivy is after the leaves are off in the fall, or before they come out again in the spring. When the boys were two and four years old, we spent a spring day hiking up Cottonwood Canyon near Point Mugu along California's southern coast. We also brought along our four-month-old Labrador Retriever. It was a warm day and we were all in short sleeves. As we proceeded up the canyon, we came to several rocky spots where the boys and dog needed help. In the absence of leaves, we didn't realize these areas were infested with poison oak. Everyone got immersed in it, but only the adults suffered the usual aftereffects. Our arms from the elbows down were covered with rash, mainly from hoisting the kids and the dog over the steep parts of the trail. Although Greg and Chris didn't break out, this does not necessarily mean that they have permanent immunity. Sooner or later most children will get poison ivy or oak if exposed.

[3] Thor Kommedahl and Herbert G. Johnson, *Pesky Plants* (Agricultural Extension Service, University of Minnesota, 1969), p. 6.

8

Camping with Care

THE TWO PLACES where man's impact on the wilderness environment is greatest are on the trail and in camp. We have already mentioned some of the considerations that will lessen your impact on the trail, like picking up after oneself and others, and preservation of existing trails. The same ethic applies to your evening camp, but even to a greater degree because your residence time will naturally be longer. If you stay at the same campsite for more than one night, the environment starts to get that "lived in" look that is difficult and sometimes impossible to irradicate. All public campgrounds and many wilderness "group" camping sites bear the unmistakable signs of overuse. Sometimes it is the usual array of tin cans, aluminum foil, or even primitive camp furniture. Other times the signs are less conspicuous—like trampled ground with a combination of campfire ashes, a few cigarette butts, and an occasional fliptop. Sooted rocks, wood chips, a piece of fishing line, and some miscellaneous disposable or supposedly biodegradable items beneath a nearby boulder further betray man's presence.

It is often the case that the accumulated evidence is not the work of a single party but due to seemingly small contributions from each of several groups using the same site over a period of time. Situations such as these may be avoided by obliterating *every* trace of your campsite. In this way, there is never any evidence to accumulate.

It is our purpose in this chapter to relate how we try to camp with care for the environment, and how children can be taught, through example, to share in this ethic. This involves choosing a campsite where your immediate impact will be least, and where even that can be erased before you leave.

Choosing a Site

In picking out a site for your temporary home you want to look for several things. Probably the most important thing you need is drinkable water. You need to camp close enough to a water source to be able to haul the water to camp without undue difficulty. This does not mean that you set your campsite two feet from the shore. There are many reasons for this. Shorelines are ecologically fragile and will not stand endless trampling. In fact, the shorelines of some lakes become so trodden that the area has to be officially closed to all camping. An example is Bullfrog Lake on the crest of the high Sierras.[1] There is also too great a danger of polluting the water when you live close to it. And you will undoubtedly scare away any fish or other creatures that live near the shore, thus lessening your chances for good fishing.

Another reason for avoiding lakesides and streamsides as camping sites is that they are dangerously inviting to children. Kids love to play in water, and if left unattended while the tent is being pitched or dinner is being prepared, a slip

[1] Ronald B. Taylor, "No Vacancy in the Wilderness," *Sierra Club Bulletin* (October–November, 1972), pp. 5–6.

could be disastrous. It is much better to choose a site a few hundred feet away from the water so that you can enjoy looking at it but will not have to worry so much about small children falling into it.

Also keep in mind that a wisely chosen site may make the difference between a cold night's sleep and a comfortable one. Cold air is heavier than warm air and therefore flows down valley at night. It will always be colder and often windier at the bottom of a valley or along a stream than on higher ground. Position your sleeping bags with your head in the downstream direction to avoid cold air flowing into them. This is particularly important for children who tend to be restess sleepers. They inevitably end up with their neck and shoulders uncovered by morning.

A final reason for avoiding camping sites near lakes and streams is that these areas harbor more insects than higher ground. A tree-lined lakeshore may look like the finest campsite on earth at 3:00 P.M., but by evening it may become intolerable because of mosquitoes. A better choice would be on rocky ground above the lake with fewer trees to take advantage of afternoon and evening breezes. Besides, a more open site means more sunlight in the evening, or if you are on the west side of the valley, more sunshine with your morning coffee.

The site should be as level as possible. It is difficult to sleep and cook on a slope. You can find a flat rock to set your stove on, but you are not about to terrace a hillside for a level tent spot. Even if you had the time, motivation, and tools, the consequence of any hillside excavation would be damaging erosion with the next rain. When sleeping it is natural for your body to roll down to the lowest level. This means that everyone ends up squashed against the lowermost tent wall making an uncomfortable night for all. Children easily slip out of their bags on a slope as they shift downhill during the night, and then mom or dad has to get up and cover them again.

Check for rocks, roots, and pinecones where the tent will be pitched. A small protuberance can become very large and uncomfortable during the night giving a "princess-and-the-pea" effect. Before we actually set up our tent, we have everyone check out their own sleeping spot. We try to have the boys take this on as a personal responsibility and tell them that mom and dad will not move over because they forgot to remove a pinecone or rock from their spots. It helps to have each person lie down on the ground in his spot before the tent goes up to see if it is level and smooth.

We encourage Greg and Chris never to remove shrubs or live roots when clearing a tent site. These changes cannot be repaired the next morning and hence should be avoided. They can temporarily remove rocks, fallen pinecones, branches, etc. for the purpose of clearing a tent site. It takes just a minute to put them back in their places when you break camp. Never cut boughs for mattresses. This permanently defaces trees. Even the revised version of the "Boy Scout Manual" agrees, reversing eons of woodcraft hacking traditions.

While checking out protuberances, keep your eyes peeled for ants, whose homes you may be disturbing. This is an important job that even the smallest child can participate in. Children love to follow ant trails and search for insects. In Norway's Telemark region we spent four summers avoiding ants while backpacking in the mountains. Their ants are huge, they build mounds two feet high, and they bite!

When choosing a site, keep in mind that in the event the weather suddenly changes, you may have to stay put for a while. As mentioned earlier, never camp on a high, exposed ridge with no trees, or just one isolated tree, because of the danger of lightning strikes during thunderstorms. If the area is above timberline, protection can be found in the form of boulders that can block the prevailing winds. Never camp at the foot of a talus slope as another rock may decide to come down while you are there. It is wise to pitch your tent in a group of trees. A grove of pines or firs may have enough space between them to set the tent. Their trunks are strong and make convenient anchors for the tent's fly ropes. Check to see that there are no dead branches overhead that could fall on someone. Pitch the back of the tent toward the prevailing wind (if confused check which way the clouds are moving). If rain accompanies the wind, you want the entrance of your tent dry and the minimum surface pelted directly by rain or hail.

A bonus to look for in choosing a tent site is that it have a naturally absorbent floor or one that will easily drain when wet. Dirt will turn to mud in a rain and track up your tent. If it is a heavy rain, and there are many afternoon or evening thundershowers, the physical impact of raindrops will splatter the splash guard and the side of your tent with mud. This happened to us once when we set up late at night in a roadside gravel pit in Alaska. We didn't know that there was a good deal of salt mixed in with the dirt and sand where we pitched the tent. That night it poured and by morning the front and sides of the tent were wet even beneath the fly. We learned months later the effects of salt. The front zipper corroded badly at the base, and the fabric eventually rotted even though the tent was dry when packed away for the winter.

A forest floor of pine needles makes for a good tent site for drainage purposes and leaves no impression of having been slept on the following morning. On several occasions we have come upon old tent sites marked only by the presence of a rectangular moatlike depression. Trenching is totally unnecessary in a natural forest floor, and should not be practiced by conscientious campers.

A broad, flat rock also makes for an ecologically sound tent site—there will be no damage to small ground-cover plants. Also, the heat absorbed by the rock in the day may come back to warm you during the night. One of the advantages of an exterior frame tent is that it can be erected directly on rock with no stakes. Guy lines for the fly can be fastened to nearby rocks. This way you leave no trace whatsoever of your tent site when you depart.

Finally, it is a matter of policy with us to police a potential campsite before we set up. If it is a previously occupied site, there will, no doubt, be bits of garbage lying around. Once these are picked up it will set the standard of how things should look when you leave. It also insures that there are no bits of broken glass or rusty metal bits lurking about to cause accidents. A fun game to play with children when you arrive at a campsite is a search for evidence of man's presence before you. It is wise to supervise this game to avoid cuts from handling cut glass, etc. When you leave, reenact the game to be sure that the next resident of the site will not spot signs of your stay.

The Question of Fire

We backpackers can no longer assume that we can start fires anywhere we choose in wilderness areas. Sheer numbers of people using such areas put heavy strains on the available firewood. Especially in higher elevations there is likely to be little windfall and dead wood lying around. The little dead wood that may exist is part of the alpine "floor" and should remain to guard against erosion. If a person scrounges for wood on existing small trees and shrubs he does irreparable damage to those plants. A fire is very difficult to start anyway with green wood. The solution is to carry a lightweight cooking stove and your own fuel. This is mandatory in some areas of the Sierras of California, as in the Sequoia–Kings Canyon National Parks wilderness areas.

Moreover, it is difficult to eradicate signs of fires. We have backpacked in areas where four or five fire rings heaped with mounds of ashes and charred cans litter a single campsite. A campsite is a temporary place to enjoy the wilderness as a

Flat rocks provide the safest and least damaging surface for cooking. Here Ann finishes up the morning dishes having heated water on the stove rather than starting a campfire.

quiet observer. We must get away from the pioneer image of subduing the wild forest, of leaving our mark. There is too little forest, too little wilderness left to us to be careless and destructive of it.

This is not to say we never use fire. We like fires in the evening just as much as anyone, and we don't like to carry ten quarts of fuel. In short, we use judgment and compromise. If we come to a site where there is plenty of dead wood lying around, there is no fire danger in the area, and we are cold, we make a small fire. We use an existing fire ring instead of making a new one. If there is none, we make our fire ring small so we can put the rocks back where we found them. You don't need a bonfire. If the fire ring is so large you can't dismantle it, it has no place in the wilderness. In the same manner, if the wood you find lying around is so large you need an axe, it shouldn't be used. An axe is too heavy to carry and is irrelevant in an ecologically concerned backpacker's pack. Large pieces of wood will not be completely consumed in the fire and will remain on the scene as chunks of charred wood.

Never cut wood off growing trees for firewood or cooking supports. This is not necessary. It is best to make a fire on an inorganic soil, sand, or rock base. Burning fires directly on the forest floor of pine needles can cause undercover smoldering, especially in peat-rich soils, resulting in possible fire eruptions later on. A meal is more simply prepared by arranging the rocks so the pots will rest on the fire ring itself. A grate is unnecessary if a pot is balanced between the rocks. There is a tendency for the stick that supports the hanging pot to become charred with the flames, which can topple the whole dinner into the fire.

After the fire is burned out, thoroughly douse the entire fire ring with water. This may require several trips to the water source. Pour the water over the rocks too, as these get

Old fire rings like this one are unsightly. Here Chris picks up after the previous residents.

hot enough to cook an egg. In the morning we normally have no fire because we want to make sure the ring is stone cold so we can disperse it. Getting rid of any trace of a fire eliminates any chance of a fire starting from old coals. When you scatter ashes with your hands you know they are cold.

There are several tricks to eradicating a fire ring and its contents so that no sign of it remains. The first is to keep the fire small with a minimum of rocks and wood. Each rock will have a soot-covered surface which should be laid fire-side down in the spot where each was found. Most rocks will have irregular shapes and thus will leave a characteristic mold in the soil from which it was taken. The bottom side of such rocks should be placed toward the fire so that when replaced the next morning, no sooted surfaces will be visible. Then take a plastic or lightweight metal trowel and scatter the few remaining ashes and charcoal discreetly about. Dense low undergrowth is a good spot providing the material is absolutely out and cold to the touch. Finally, scatter fresh soil or sand over the firesite so it looks as close as possible to the terrain as you first encountered it.

It is assumed that any backpacker will be exceedingly careful with fire. It poses a great threat to plant and animal life. Some dry areas may forbid fires altogether. Some areas require permits. This information can be obtained from the forest service offices. Once on a seven-day trip we paused for lunch on a ridge where there was a good view of a fire scar. The charred trunks extended for several hundred acres, and there were no birds or animals to be seen. Greg never really understood that fires kill animals and plants until that moment. It made quite an impression on him.

Fires are also a potential hazard to young children who are fascinated by the flickering flames. Careful supervision is needed around the campfire so that young children don't inadvertently stumble into it or get singed by an odd-flying spark. You must also take care that your fire is downwind of your tent. Most backpacking tents are constructed of synthetic material that is quite flammable. A stray spark can easily singe a hole in your fly or tent that will be a real nuisance when it rains. Down-filled nylon or Dacron parkas are equally vulnerable, especially when worn by a small child who is trying to warm up next to the fire.

Sanitary Considerations

In most established campgrounds, forest service or other, the reek of the pit toilets overpowers the natural forest odors. Little can be done about this. It simply reflects the increased popularity of camping.

The alternative is an isolated site in the backcountry where there are no centralized pit toilets. One of the most important problems backpackers must face is how to handle this primitive bathroom situation. There are no available outhouses in most wilderness areas. If there are, use them. Most of the time, however, it is between you and the bushes.

Of all the things man leaves behind on his journeys through the wilderness, nothing is more biodegradable than his own excrement. In this respect, man does not differ from the wild animals around him. But man, being the fastidious creature he is, insists upon leaving other less biodegradable signs behind of his natural functions. There is nothing more disgusting than to come upon a campsite where bits of toilet paper and tissue paper are scattered about under bushes. Even in more respectable sites we are somewhat reluctant to remove rocks for anchoring guy lines for fear of finding yet another piece of toilet paper lurking underneath.

Such littering is inexcusable, and can easily be avoided. The U.S. Forest Service advocates burial of excrement and toilet paper in a hole six to eight inches deep and at least fifty feet away from an open water source. Eventually nature will do its work providing there is sufficient water and aeration for decomposition. In arid, rocky areas, especially above timberline, the time required for decomposition of toilet paper is far longer than the few days commonly advertised. In the meantime everyone and his neighbor will have the opportunity to discover your leavings. Rodents also help out. They have not the least aversion to digging up your used paper for all to see.

Therefore, rule number one in our family is don't bury toilet paper, or stash it behind a rock or bush. We carry a plastic bag just for this purpose. When Greg and Chris finish their business we insist they bring back their paper. This is then toted to the campfire and burned, or if no fire is being used we put it in a plastic bag to be either hauled out or burned later when we do have a fire.

Rule number two is bury the stool. We carry a lightweight aluminum garden trowel for this very purpose. Just dig the small hole a few inches deep, do your business in the hole, and cover it back up with the dirt. If moss was growing on the spot, put it back as you would a divot on a golf course. If a rock was there, just replace it. Human droppings, buried properly, leave no trace or odor to offend the next party coming through. It is also considerate to do one's business several hundred feet away from a possible campsite, trail, or water source so there is little likelihood of its discovery. At first young children need to be helped with finding an out of the way spot, digging their hole, and replacing the dirt. It seems silly to give instructions for what cats do naturally, but we have found enough toilet paper in the years that we have been backpacking to know that this type of behavior is not instinctive among humans.

For a longer stay or a larger party, one spot should be chosen as a latrine and a larger hole dug for common use, then covered and restored to original appearance when it is time to leave. It is unnecessary to surround the whole campsite with bush stops. If the area has little rain, it is conceivable that the site could start smelling after a couple of days. Hopefully, your stay will not be prolonged, nor your party large, for such is not the best use of wilderness areas.

Camp Routines

By now the camp should be comfortable. You have established a level place for the tent and erected it. A small fire ring is carefully built with the idea that it will be dismantled later. The trowel is out. Small pieces of dead wood are collected for a fire. Someone can fetch water and start preparing dinner.

It is a good idea to air sleeping bags and pads when you arrive at your destination. They are more comfortable and much warmer when they achieve maximum loft. They also smell nicer when aired regularly. Ideally, they should be aired out in the morning before departure also. The late afternoon airing is good as long as there is no moisture in the air. If there is a hint of rain, fluff the bags in the tent.

Clothes washing is easily done after the dinner dishes are put away. (See Chapter 6.) Someone can start gathering up the dirty clothes for washing, especially socks. Do some footsoaking in the lake while dinner is cooking. How good it feels to have dry, clean socks and clean feet to put into them after hiking all day!

Sometimes our boys like to help with these camp routines, but mostly they like to play and do what they want. A good campsite game for them is finding little twigs and sticks to use as lincoln logs. They have made real masterpieces out of them. Above timberline, stones make good building materials. Cabins, churches, factories, castles, suddenly appear—all holding the interest of their small builders for awhile. These natural toys are great for when parents are fixing dinner or just wanting some quiet relaxation after the day's hiking. The sticks might be used in the fire when the game grows old.

When finished cooking it is sometimes a problem what to do with the grease. Grease dumped on the ground will attract animals. Besides, it looks terrible. We never have this problem now, as our large Labrador loves any kind of leftovers on his kibble. If you don't have such a walking garbage disposal, bury grease, dish water or other refuse in a hole and cover it up well. Be sure to wash and rinse dishes well away from your water source.

Paper garbage can be burned in the small fire in the evening. Plastic food bags can be used for storing nonburnable trash, as aluminum foil food wrapping and plastics which can be packed out later. Never leave such nonbiodegradable garbage lying around. Do not bury it either, for it will not decompose, and, as with toilet paper, animals will dig it up.

While in camp you must take the usual safety precautions you would take in your home against kitchen dangers for small children. There are no kitchen drawers in which to place sharp knives, so there is a tendency to leave them on top of a rock or log while the meal is prepared. We usually have nothing more than a pocketknife, and its safest location out of reach of small hands is obvious.

Other camp precautions include keeping children away from gas stoves. Our little Svea 123 puts out intense heat when properly primed. It can be easily heard when operating but in daylight, with the windscreen up, the flame is not readily seen. The metal parts become exceedingly hot. Take care also to keep fuel containers out of reach of the stove and children. White gas is highly explosive.

Breaking Camp

Most of what is involved in breaking camp has already been mentioned. The whole idea is to leave the camp as you found it, or better than you found it. Police the site for any garbage you can find to pack out, even if it is not your own. Do not burn it just before leaving as you will want to disperse the fire ring, and it should be cold to the touch. As

After dinner and the camp chores are completed, everyone looks forward to a marshmallow and a story before going to bed.

mentioned, we do not usually have a fire in the morning for this reason, unless we are having a delayed departure around noontime. Scatter the used rocks, burned sides down in their old niches. Scatter unused wood about. Scatter the cold ashes with your hands so you know they are dead. Replenish fireplace with moss or pine needles or other natural material.

After airing and packing sleeping bags and pads, shake out the tent and let the bottom dry before rolling it up. Then scruff up the area where the tent was with your boot. The weight of the people in the tent packs down the grass pretty flat. Things should look pretty good now for the next party to "discover."

9
Extended Trips

AFTER ALL THE PLANNING and preparation have gone into the first backpacking trip, which often by necessity is a short overnight or three-day trip, there is a real urge to do a longer one. It usually takes at least a day just to get away from the highways, campgrounds, and other people. It seems a shame to have to turn around and head back home after finally reaching a wilderness site. Once a short trip has been completed successfully, longer trips from four to seven days and then even ten days to two weeks can be planned with confidence. The goal should be a long enough trip to make all those preparations worth the effort. More importantly, it is only through a long trip that one can get far enough into the wilderness to be able to appreciate its solitude and beauty.

Assuming there is time and motivation for a longer backpacking trip, the specific number of days you can manage with a child will largely depend on how well your child can walk. Another factor of less importance is the nature of the area to be visited. The basic premise here is that the child who does not have to be carried frees a parent's back for more food, thus extending the trip. Similarly, the fewer

When the day is done, who could ask for a snugger home than a sleeping bag and tent?

clothes changes that have to be carried the more room there is in the pack for food giving you more days on the trail.

Any outing must be geared down to the youngest's hiking ability. Our first real backpacking trips of three to five days in length were taken when Chris was almost two and Greg was almost four. We planned routes in the Sierra Nevada's eastern high country, which is notoriously dry but with lakes averaging two miles apart—ideal backpacking country for those who do not wish to cover many miles each day. Our first trip was out of Onion Valley near the town of Independence. The first day we hiked two miles with a 1,000-foot vertical rise. The third day, on the way out, we descended 2,000 vertical feet over a distance of four miles. We did another trip later that summer out of South Lake near Bishop, California, with similar mileage but extended it to five days. We had hot, sunny weather, and all of us enjoyed it immensely.

These experiences encouraged us to try longer trips the next summer when the boys were almost three and five. We discovered the boys enjoyed trips in the five- to nine-day range. By the tenth day everyone had had enough and was ready to come back to civilization. Mileage per day increased by a couple of miles. Chris could manage five or six miles at a maximum but preferred doing less. Greg could have hiked much farther and enjoyed it, but we were careful to scale the trip to Chris's ability. We also found we could not do five miles each day. If we did five miles one day, the next day we would only do two, or hike for half a day. Then the next day, we might be able to do five again.

It may be helpful for the prospective backpacking family to see how some actual trips worked for us. In the summer just mentioned we had the opportunity to take three backpacking trips from three days to ten days in length. We decided that the Bridger Wilderness area in western Wyoming would be interesting to explore. It would be an alpine area, so there would be little to worry about in the way of snakes, poison oak, or other nasties often found at lower elevations. It was supposed to be very beautiful, and best of all, it was reportedly less crowded than other alpine areas we had visited such as portions of the Sierras. We wrote to Pinedale, Wyoming, in care of the district U.S. Forest Service office to obtain the necessary trail maps. We also ordered topographic maps of the area from the U.S. Geological Survey office in Denver, Colorado. We decided we would try to see as much of the Bridger Wilderness in the six weeks' time we had, working north to south.

Green River Lake Trip

Our first trip was in the northern end of the wilderness out of Green River Lake. This involved a long drive on a dirt road some fifty-two miles out of Pinedale, our stocking up

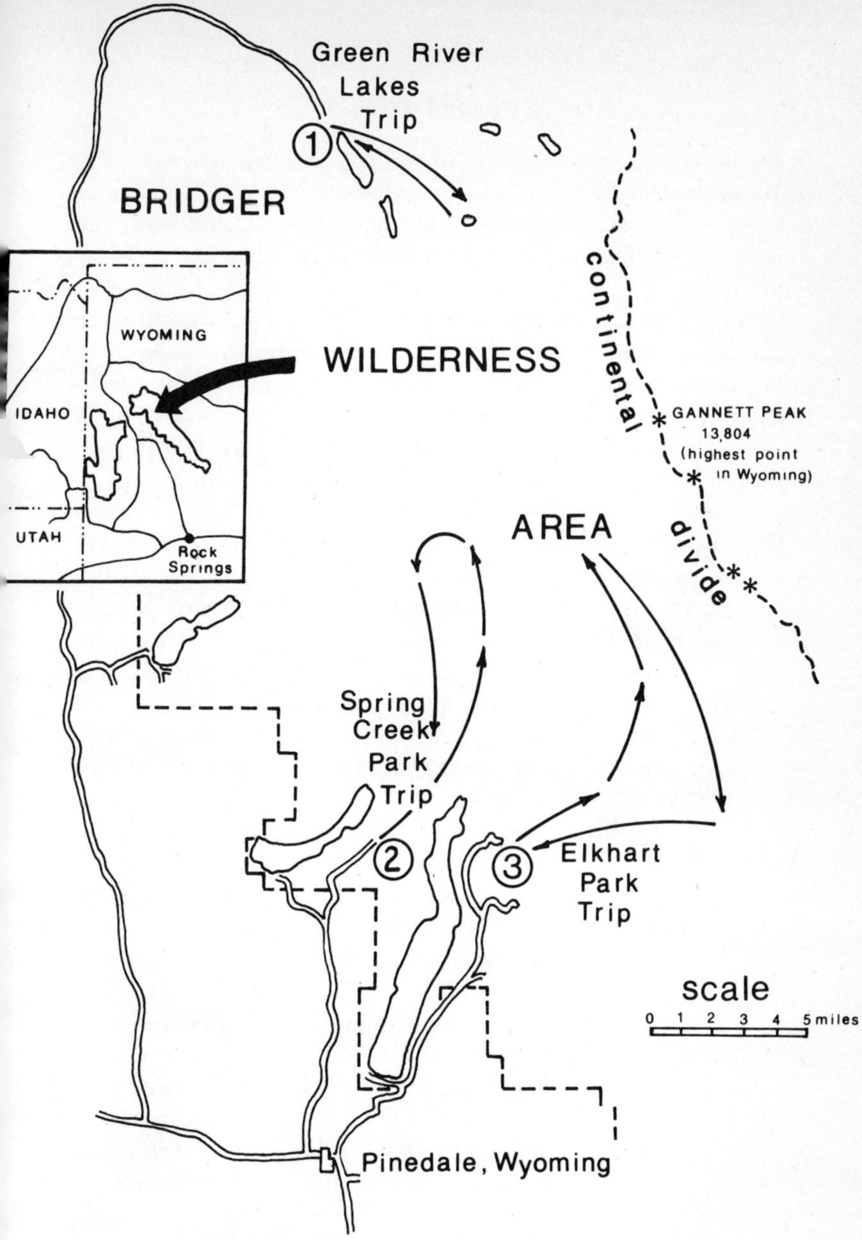

Three routes we explored in the Bridger Wilderness area in western Wyoming.

place for the next six weeks. It was our first backpacking trip of the summer, and we were all anxious to try on our packs and get going. We were also anticipating a reunion with the Adamses, old friends from California who also had a small boy Chris's age.

Our packs were loaded, and it was a beautiful day to start. Jim's pack weighed in at a reasonable forty-three pounds, Ann's at twenty-three, Greg's at four pounds, and Chris with a token one pound. Greg and Chris needed no prodding as they vigorously hiked along the level trail that followed Green River Lake. The novelty of the backpacking experience was enough to keep them going.

By lunchtime it had clouded up considerably, but it was still hot enough to have a wade in the shallow end of the lake. The water in the lake was quite cold, making a delicious and refreshing cold drink when mixed with instant lemonade. The boys enjoyed playing in the sand and finding interesting pieces of dried wood on the beach.

By 1:00 or so it was time to load up again. There was a three-hundred-foot climb ahead, and the enthusiasm waned a little. Chris enjoyed holding someone's hand going uphill. We had to stop frequently until he felt like going on again. After about an hour we got to the top of the climb, and it leveled out once more. Almost immediately, both boys increased their pace and even started running. They really moved along then because they could see way ahead and could move easier and faster.

It didn't take very much longer to get to the intersection of Clear and Slide creeks, our intended campsite. The creeks meandered happily through level meadows before they started their journey downhill to Green River Lake. Here and there were little raised portions of land above the creek with trees and shrubs. It was on one such little hill that we made our camp.

The rain had managed to hold off so far. Everyone was in good spirits. The trout were jumping, and the boys were quite excited to try some fishing. They were not disap-

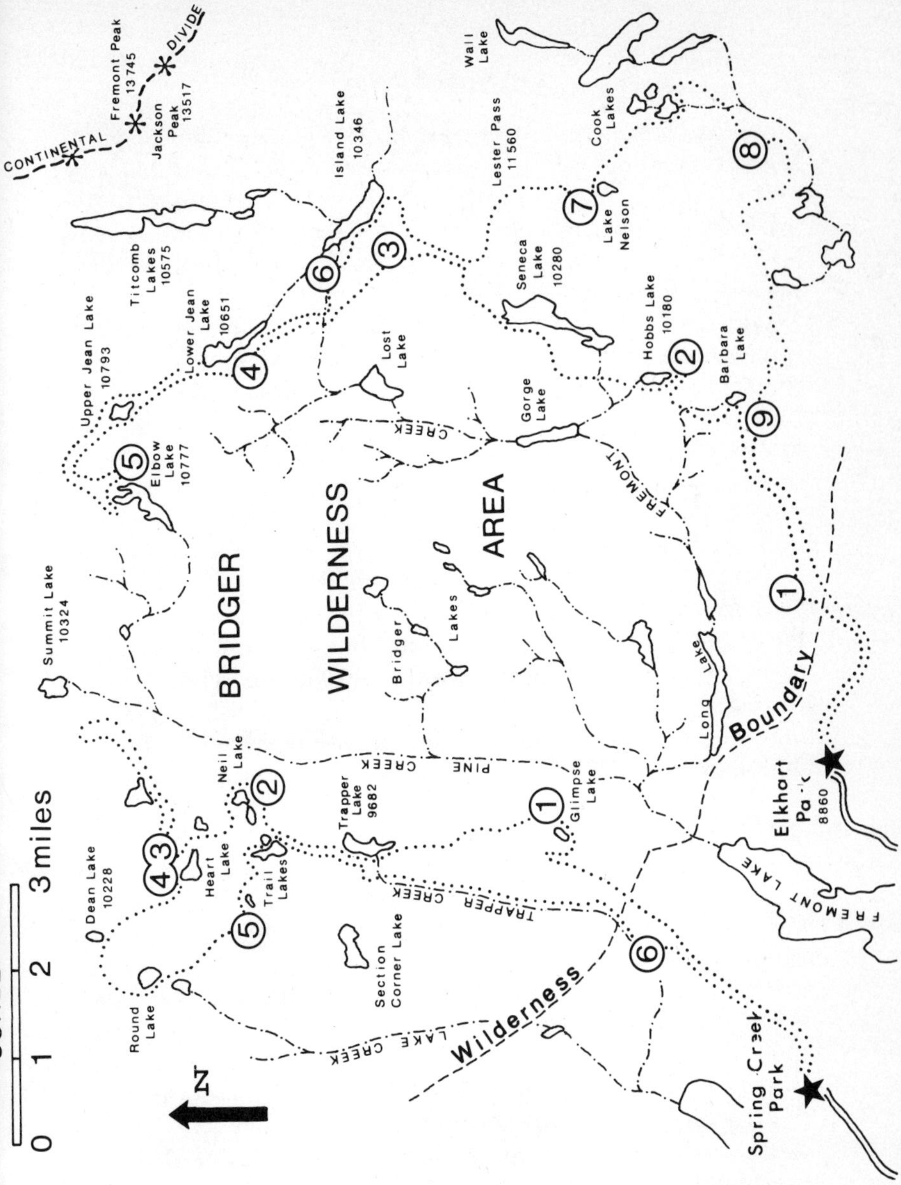

Routes (dotted lines) for Spring Creek Park and Elkhart Park trips. Campsites are numbered consecutively for each trip. Adapted from Bridger National Forest map, Bridger Wilderness unit 3, 1971.

pointed. There were many trout in the stream, and they were not very clever. With help each boy managed to land his very own.

That evening we tested our theory that we would all fit in our two-man mountain tent. It was crowded, but we all—including our Labrador—slept comfortably.

The next morning dawned partly cloudy, but not terribly threatening, so we decided to have a day hike up to the top of the next ridge to try the fishing up there. The goal was Slide Lake, one and one-half miles distant with an eight-hundred-foot vertical rise. We departed at 10:00 A.M. with rain gear, lunch, and fishing equipment in the small packs. We also included the first-aid kit, a flashlight, matches, and emergency rations in the event we were delayed. Before we left camp we made certain the storm flaps on the tent were zipped shut. We also made a last check on the guylines for the rain fly. With thunderheads developing before noon, we wanted to be certain a dry home would be waiting when we returned.

It took two hours to reach the top, taking time out for numerous views of Slide Creek sliding down toward our campsite below.

After lunch the clouds developed into obvious thunderheads. We knew that it would only take an hour to reach the campsite as it was all downhill, so we decided to investigate this higher meadow for fishing. It turned out to be fantastic. A size 12 Adams drew a hit on nearly every cast. All the trout were in the eight- to twelve-inch range with dazzling orange and white undersides and white and black tipped fins.

By 4:00 P.M. we had caught enough fish for dinner, and there were some drops starting to come down. We hustled down the trail to our camp in our rain gear and waited out the brief but thorough storm in our tents. By 6:00 the sun was out again. The foliage gleamed, its wetness reflected by the setting sun. It was too damp to sit on the ground, but the children found several logs—seats for our outdoor trout feast. We were very glad we had brought our Svea stove as the available wood was still quite wet.

The next day brought many clouds with threat of more rain. There was really no point in extending the trip with the weather so uncertain. We had food for another day due to the fish we had eaten instead of the freeze-dried food, but we decided it would be wise to get back to the car in case a regional storm was developing.

All went smoothly on the downhill section (the one that had slowed us up two days earlier) before Green River Lake. Then it started to rain as we had lunch, and we all took refuge under some firs. Fortunately it cleared up after an hour or so, making the return trip a dry one. It got almost too hot, and again the boys' enthusiasm lagged. Chris, particularly, seemed to delight in teasing us. He scuffed along, sat in the trail, played with sand, and did everything but hike in the desired direction along the trail. The novelty of hiking had worn off again. It was hot; he was tired. At this point we had to stop and just let him play. To get him going after a drink and a snack we had Greg challenge him to a "motorboat" race. That motivated him finally. We even had trouble keeping up with them after that. Although the total distance back to the car that day was only about two miles, the boys seemed tired from the hiking they had done the past two days.

We were all glad to get back to the car and our base camp. We all had a fresh cold drink, a snack, and enjoyed relaxing. The children, to our surprise and pleasure, recovered immediately. They proceeded to tear around the camp as if they had had no exercise for a week!

We were pleased that we had set a goal geared to children, and that we had been able to carry it out successfully. We were also pleased that we had had such good luck fishing and had so much food left over. We felt confident that the boys would enjoy a longer trip as long as we rested a couple of days. We planned to take one after a day or two. It would take the better part of a day to return to Pinedale, get supplies, do a laundry, and check the mail.

The next afternoon we said good-by to our friends, and headed for the nearest public showers! With that done we were ready to plan our next trip.

Spring Creek Park

Our next trip was to be out of Spring Creek Park, an entrance to the Bridger Wilderness area just north of Fremont Lake. We chose this entrance because it provided a gradual ascent of the range, and, because of its newness at that time, it was supposed to be less used than the more popular accesses to the south.

On the road into Spring Creek Park we found out why packers did not trailer in their horses. Our VW bus just squeezed over several rocky and steep portions of the road, and at the high altitude our fifty-five horsepower engine was really working overtime. The sign at the Bridger National Forest boundary indicated two miles to our trailhead, but it seemed more like three or four miles. The great white thunderheads which had been forming since noon now had coalesced into a dark gray, even black sky that promised to dump late afternoon rain. We were particularly anxious to reach our destination before the rain as the dirt road would then be impassable.

We arrived at the trailhead by 5:00 P.M. with claps of thunder around us. Shortly after the tents were pitched and rain flies were secured (we use two mountain tents when we are car-camping) the first drops came. The ensuing rain mixed with hail delayed our dinner an hour, but as usual, the rain subsided and the skies cleared. While Ann was preparing the long awaited dinner, Jim began assembling gear for the trip. We then discovered that the brass burner plate on our Svea stove was missing! The stove would not work properly without it, and the prospects of returning down the muddy, steep road to pick up the piece in Pinedale seemed quite discouraging. Finally Jim thought of fashioning the piece out of the end of a tin can found nearby. That was the first time someone else's litter paid off! He successfully cut the can end to the proper shape with small scissors so that it fit the stove exactly. We tried out the arrangement and were relieved to find that it worked fine.

The boys had no trouble falling asleep that night. They had been most helpful after the rain stopped. Their job had been to find dry wood lying around under the many wet pieces on the ground. By the time we got them to bed it was after 9:00, and there was no point in groping around in the dark to load our packs. We did grease all the boots around the fire, though, and then turned in ourselves.

During the night there was crashing in the woods from a large animal. Visions of a bear or an elk running berserk appeared in our minds, but vanished quickly with the plaintive wail of a lost cow.

In the morning we were busy checking the last details of equipment and food. We did not get the packs loaded until 10:30. They were heavier this time: Jim's weighing almost fifty pounds, Ann's over thirty, and the boys' about the same as the last trip. We planned on a seven-day trip, and the increase in weight was the extra food that had to be carried.

Our destination was Glimpse Lake, six miles distant according to the trailhead sign. We signed in, put on the packs, and stepped out into the morning sun. It appeared that the storms were finally spent and that things were going to dry out. There were no clouds anywhere.

The trail was to gradually wend its way up a long ridge (about 1,000 feet of vertical rise), skirt a ridge overlooking Fremont Lake, and finally drop down to Glimpse Lake, a couple of hundred feet below. We were all in high spirits as we hiked. The trail was in good condition and cool under the pines. It was never steep, just pleasant. Chris was a constant chatterbox all morning, talking about everything from black butterflies to Santa Claus. We saw elk tracks and droppings on the trail, which provided additional topics of conversation—all the while we were progressing steadily uphill.

We took a ten-minute break on the ridge after a half hour of hiking through mixed pine and cottonwood. What a spectacular view! Fremont Lake lay at our feet, and the view to the southern part of the Bridger Wilderness must have extended for one hundred miles—a far cry from the polluted skyline of the crowded city!

We pushed on. Chipmunks, squirrels, grasshoppers, and more elk tracks highlighted the morning until we again came out onto the edge of the ridge overlooking Fremont Lake. This time we also had a view of Long Lake and the backcountry we were heading for. We figured we had climbed about 1,000 feet from the 8,300-foot elevation where we started at Spring Creek Park and that we had come about three miles or halfway. It was high time for lunch. We had to ration our water as it did not look like we were going to come across any for awhile.

After lunch we were all refreshed and continued on. The trail rose gradually, unrelentingly. Soon it leveled off again, and there was a major fork in the trail. It was unmarked. Ann went on the south trail leaving Jim with the boys. She returned quickly, reporting that it just dropped down toward the east end of Fremont Lake, several hundred feet below. So we proceeded on the northerly trail, always up and always east. We were beginning to think we had chosen a trail that was too long for the boys. We had to stop frequently. It was good we had as many lemon drops as we did. What with the shortage of water, they really came in handy.

Finally by 4:00 we could see the trail's descent to a sizable lake several hundred feet down. As we approached the pretty lake we had the feeling we were the first people to set eyes upon it. There was no camp in evidence anywhere around the lake. The concentric rings on the lake surface promised good fishing. We found a good, level site about one hundred feet from the north side of the lake. Just then Chris discovered two Olympia beer cans stuck between the lower branches of a fir. Then Greg spotted a beer bottle half-submerged in the lake. To top it off there was a huge fire ring thirty feet away littered with a variety of charred cans and bottles. Dried horse manure was here and there betraying the previous residents. It is highly unlikely that backpackers could have managed to carry up all those heavy cans and bottles. The least the party on horseback could have done was to pack out all the garbage that they packed in. We did the best we could to tidy up the area, placing the bulk of the cans and bottles in a neat pile near the trail in the hope that the trail crews or another party on horseback could pack it out. We do not start toting other people's garbage until we are on the way out with lightened packs.

We had the entire lake to ourselves until the next morning when a moose appeared on the opposite side of the lake. We watched it feed on water plants for nearly half an hour. About 9:30 we packed up and headed for Trapper Lake and beyond.

At Trapper Lake there is a convergence of trails. The piles of horse manure and the broad dusty trail was evidence of the popularity of pack animals. We were further disturbed by the sight of a trailbike track. They are not allowed in wilderness areas.

There were at least three parties camped at Trapper Lake, which was too many to suit us. It was still early in the afternoon, so we pushed on another mile to Neil Lake. It was time to stop. The total distance we had traveled that day was only about three miles, but we were all somewhat tired from the long day before. The sky also looked ominous again, so we flied the tent in preparation for possible rain. We were higher than the last night, and the trees were smaller and farther apart. There were cutthroat trout in the lake. It was very pleasant until the wind died down just before dinnertime. Then it seemed as if Neil Lake was the breeding ground for half of the mosquitoes in the Wind Rivers! We all put on our hooded windbreakers and smeared on mosquito repellent.

After dinner they got worse than ever, and we all retreated into the tent.

About midnight Chris woke and demanded his blanket. He had not missed it at all the previous night at Glimpse Lake, but now he was determined to have it. We explained that he was a big boy and no longer needed his "blankie." The message got through only to the extent that he changed the conditions of his demand—he now wanted a second bottle of milk, which had been readied earlier and which we hoped would put him asleep again. As soon as the last drop of milk disappeared, Chris demanded his blanket with even more vigor than before. With the milk supply exhausted, we turned again to reasoning. We reminded Chris that his sleeping bag was soft and warm and cuddly just like his blanket with even more warmth for the mountains. To even suggest that a bag of feathers was in any way superior to his blanket was to arouse more cries! Finally, the long day caught up with him, and we all went back to sleep again.

The next day we decided that Heart Lake would make a good base camp from which to explore the surrounding territory. Heart Lake, being just over 10,000 feet, was somewhat higher than Neil Lake, which we hoped would alleviate the mosquito problem. In a couple of hours we were there. It was a lovely spot, and we were content to set up camp and hike and fish for the rest of the day close to camp. It rained that night but we stayed warm and dry in our tent. We decided to camp at Heart Lake for the next day but take a day hike up to Summit Lake and back just to see what the country looked like.

This was to prove an exercise of sheer delight because we left our big packs behind for this excursion. One advantage of getting into the backcountry and remaining for several days is that you can set up a base camp from which day hikes can be taken. After toting a home on your back for several days, you can really appreciate walking without it for a change.

We took Greg's small pack and frame to hold our lunch and rain gear. We anticipated that we might return late in the afternoon so we threw in our down shirts in case we cooled off, the usual first-aid kit, emergency ration, and a flashlight. The main trail up to Summit Lake turned out to be a real mire after the previous night's rain. On top of that, two pack trains ahead of us were making a real mess out of the trail. Portions of grassy meadows became bogs under the weight of the heavily laden pack animals, and the rest of the trail was a challenge as we attempted to rock hop between mud holes. Because of the poor condition of the trail we took to the rocks and better drained terrain off to one side. This led to a long, rocky ridge that proved much more interesting to the boys than the quagmire below us. At the end of the ridge we ate lunch overlooking Summit Lake. From there we could see north toward Green River Lake where we had been earlier and south to the beautiful crest of the Wind Rivers where we would be venturing several days later. This vantage point offered a new view of the Bridger Wilderness that we had not as yet experienced. We were impressed with the vastness of it all. This escaped us at lower elevations where the terrain was more gentle and trees were abundant. But here there was hardly a tree to be seen. In their place were lovely shades of white, gray, and black that stretched for as far as we could see. From off in the distance came the isolated whistle of a marmot. It was nice to know that such places still existed.

We spent the remainder of the day in leisure just wandering around several alpine meadows basking in the sun. After a short afternoon nap, we headed back for camp. That evening we tried our luck fly casting for some hefty rainbow trout that suddenly went on an eating spree. Breakfast was secured in less than an hour. In the process, Chris appeared on the scene minus one boot. Both boys had come close to losing hats and even sunglasses on previous days, but never an item so essential as a boot. We immediately dropped everything and launched a full-scale search in quest of the lost boot. Twenty feet away we found it—right in the middle of the trail.

Catching a few beauties like these makes extended trips possible.

The next morning we headed north toward Dean Lake to start the loop back to the trailhead. The trail rose a few hundred feet to several high meadows. The climb with the morning sun to our backs really warmed us up. Greg and Chris were brimming with energy, and we needed only one rest stop the entire way up. We felt as if we were finally getting in good shape. The lighter packs plus rest the previous day helped.

Once through the high meadows, the trail dropped down to a different type of terrain. Here the country was open with only patches of firs scattered here and there. Instead of the barren gray rock we had encountered at higher elevation, here everything was covered with grass and low-lying shrubs. By noon thunderheads had billowed up to the south. Two hours later we made a run for it across a huge meadow to a grove of sheltering firs. For nearly an hour we remained there as the skies rumbled and lightning flashed.

The rest of the afternoon brought many small, marshy lakes and ill-marked trails that seemed to wander about aimlessly. We finally concluded that we had strayed from the main trail. By 5:00 P.M. we came to a very shallow lake teeming with small grayling. We were ready to stop for the day. The skies were threatening rain again and we wanted to confirm our location before morning. When we took this trip there were no topographic maps available for this particular area. We had only the forest service trail maps which proved adequate but on which it is sometimes difficult to locate oneself. Without contour lines the size and shape of lakes are often helpful for locating your position. If there are not high spots free of trees from where you can get an overview, the direction the lake, or one side of it, trends is often sufficient for positive identification.

That evening before the rain came, the boys had a fantastic time catching grayling. The unnamed lake was so overpopulated with them that there was no fish longer than about seven inches. That made no difference to the boys. The fish were so eager that a bedraggled black gnat tied on a barbless hook could turn the water to a frenzy. By 8:00 P.M. the boys were fast asleep. We heard not even a peep from them the whole night through, even though we were woken several times by great crashes of thunder and bright lightning.

A short hike the next morning brought us to Trail Lakes, only a short distance from the main trail we had come in on. We arrived at Trapper Lake by noon where we had to make a decision.

We spent our sixth night along Trapper Creek. We could have made it back to Spring Creek Park and our car by evening. But the boys were taking such great delight in playing along the sandbars on Trapper Creek that we decided to hike the last few miles the next morning.

We reached the trailhead parking area by 11:00 the next day. A rude shock awaited us. Jim turned the key in the ignition; there was no response. It seemed impossible that there could be a dead battery. We had checked the lights and radio before we left seven days earlier, but somehow the radio had not been turned off completely. It was not turned up enough to be audible, just enough to be on. The battery was completely dead. There wasn't a soul around. There was only a lone pickup truck. Its party had just left that morning on a ten-day trip according to the register. After several attempts to push the car downhill in an effort to start it, we gave up. The huge boulders in the road blocked any kind of a roll we could have achieved on a normal road. After some discussion we borrowed the battery from the pickup, drove to town to recharge our own, and then returned immediately to replace it. We learned a good lesson. The last thing to do before locking the car up is to systematically check that the radio and lights are off. In case of an emergency, you don't want to discover a dead battery.

Elkhart Park

For our last foray into the Wind Rivers we decided we would try a ten-day trip. We were curious to see if the boys would enjoy being out that long. The biggest problem was how to carry enough food for that length of time. We decided we could not carry any more than we had for the seven-day trip. Our fishing luck on the past two trips had been so good that we anticipated being able to supplement our diet with trout or grayling. We would evaluate our food supply as we went along to see when we should turn back. The more fish we could catch, the longer we could stay.

The time we had for backpacking was running short, so we decided against spending a whole day in Pinedale. It seemed silly to spend another night in the local, private campground when all we needed were showers. Besides, we had no desire to sandwich in between trailers and campers when we could sleep between pines.

We were anxious to see the section of the Wind Rivers out

of Elkhart Park. This entrance has trails leading to the highest peaks in Wyoming. Gannett Peak at 13,804 feet heads a whole string of impressive mountains all over 13,500 feet. These peaks are part of the continental divide and are spectacular from fifty miles away. We were looking forward to getting a closer look at them.

By the time we ate lunch, drove to the trailhead, signed in, and loaded our packs, it was already 2:00 P.M. It wasn't the best hour of the day to start, but we decided we would try it anyway. The map showed the first lake five miles distant, which was impossible for us to make in a couple of hours, so we carried extra water and planned to stop where we found an appropriate spot.

It was a good thing we had not planned a long afternoon on the trail. The kids lost their enthusiasm after we had gone a mile or so. It was then we discovered that Chris no longer had his hat. It wasn't to be seen anywhere. "Where is your hat?" we asked. He replied, "I don't like it. I threw it 'way." Back down the trail trudged Jim about a quarter of a mile to retrieve the hat. It was a good lesson. Children of two or three years of age have a very short attention span. Chris can be holding his hat or dark glasses as he walks along a trail, and as soon as he spies something of interest he just drops everything and continues on. Hats and sunglasses are important items at high altitude, so extra care must be taken to insure that they are not lost.

The trials of the afternoon were just beginning. Both boys were more intent on dragging small logs, throwing dirt, or stirring fresh horse manure with sticks than hiking up the trail. The standard ploys were of no avail. Even "bye-bye" and heading out of sight did not work. Lemon drops worked for about five minutes, but Chris soon dropped his into a horsetrodden quagmire which did nothing to improve his disposition. On top of that Greg seemed to get a sadistic satisfaction, as he does on occasion, from hearing Chris scream with displeasure. Greg went so far as to remind Chris that he could not have his bottle of milk until after dinner, and the final straw was that we had left Chris's blanket in the car. Just as we would get everyone set straight and moving along the trail, one of them would announce that it was time for a "doo doo."

In addition to the problems we were having on the trail, the weather was not cooperating. Thunder in the distance got closer, and by 5:00 it appeared that we were in for a storm. We headed for the first grove of trees and sat out half an hour. We were thankful we had thought to bring extra water. There was none around, and we could not go any farther that day.

When the rain stopped, and the sun reappeared, we peered out into the alpine meadow from our protective grove of firs. The late afternoon sun's rays caught the raindrops still on the grasses and wildflowers making the whole scene sparkle. To the east, high peaks dominated the horizon. We were glad we had come. The difficulties of the afternoon were forgotten in the calm and freshness of the evening. We spotted a young red fox. He was in the meadow hunting small rodents.

The next day dawned with no clouds. It turned out that Barbara Lake, the next water source, was about three miles from where we had camped the night before. Our destination for the day had been Seneca Lake, but that proved impossible for us, as it was farther by two miles than the map indicated. We headed for Hobbs Lake which was only about a mile past Barbara, making the total for the day about four miles.

Hobbs Lake was one of our favorite spots on the whole trip. Barely within timberline, its waters were beautifully clear. The site offered a splendid view of the high country we were approaching. We encountered more wildlife here. As we dug into the cook kit to get out the pots, out jumped a little gray mouse! He had chewed up some paper towels that had been tucked inside. No doubt he thought they would make a nice nest! The boys were delighted to see the little fellow, although they had only a quick look. The mouse quickly scurried under the nearest rock and never appeared again. We wondered what he would do after having been moved four miles from his previous home.

As it was a Sunday, and we were on the most popular trail in the Wind Rivers, we were not too surprised at the large numbers of people on the trail. Large pack trains, families, boy scout troops, and climbing parties passed by on their way to Island Lake and the high country. We had decided earlier to avoid the crowds and visit Elbow Lake, on a different loop and out of the usual route.

The next day again dawned clear. It is hard to describe the delights of eating freshly caught trout and hash browns (even the freeze-dried ones are surprisingly good) in the morning sun with splendid views all around! The boys' appetites were just as cavernous as ours. We had no trouble consuming nine large trout.

After letting the breakfast settle and the clothes dry that had been washed, we set off at a leisurely pace. The scenery grew more and more rocky as we gained elevation. Seneca Lake, where we stopped for lunch, was beautifully blue, clear, and deep. Jim caught two rainbow trout each about seventeen inches long. These we placed in a tightly sealed plastic bag deep in the pack where they would remain cool for the remainder of the day.

After Seneca Lake the terrain became even rockier and very irregular with many ridges to climb over. It was on one such ridge that we passed a man resting. He was a member of a large party that had gone ahead on horseback. He had decided to hike instead but was having second thoughts about it all. He looked in surprise at the boys and asked how old they were. "I can't believe it!" he exclaimed upon hearing they were both under five. He surged by a few minutes later, but in about an hour we passed him by again. As he rested against a rock, we heard him saying over and over again, "I just can't believe it, I don't believe it."

We made camp on a rise overlooking a small stream that night. There was plenty of dry wood around, but we could see that this would be our last fire for awhile. We had packed two quarts of fuel knowing we would be above timberline for several days. As the last coals flickered out, we gazed with wonder at the incredible number of stars in the sky. It was something we rarely saw in the city.

A perfectly clear sky greeted us as we woke the next morning. We had chosen our campsite on the east side of the slope in order to catch the sun's first rays in the morning. We forgot, however, that the crest of the Wind River Range towering above us to the east would catch the morning sun first. We were so close to the divide that the sun didn't reach us til midmorning. The boys were up by then and had a fun time watching the shadow of the mountains retreat across our camp as the sun appeared.

Soon we were off again. The trail led north across some lovely mixed rock and meadow terrain and then dropped down to Fremont Crossing. We had seen the name on our map but did not realize that it was a full-sized wooden bridge across Fremont Creek. It was large enough to support an entire pack train. It seemed strangely out of place, but also very convenient. Fremont Creek comes as a small river out of Island Lake to the south, and a crossing by foot would be perilous with small children. When we had planned our general route a month earlier, Fremont Creek caught our attention as a potentially dangerous crossing. Without the bridge it certainly would have been.

The afternoon found us well above timberline. We were suddenly at the very base of the great peaks we had been looking at from a distance for the previous three days. The last trees were far below us. The gray expanses of rock stretched for miles and miles, broken only by the cobalt blue sky. This was new and unfamiliar terrain. Greg and Chris took to it quickly. They loved climbing the huge outcrops of granite. We had talked to a group of young climbers the day before who were heading down after climbing Gannett Peak. The boys were awed by their ropes, crampons, and ice axes. Now climbing was even more interesting to them than before. They were taking on boulders that were so rugged that we found it necessary to give them constant attention. This became apparent when Chris screamed for help. He was stuck halfway up a rock about six feet from the ground. It was too steep to go higher, and he couldn't maneuver back down. That is where he learned that it is sometimes easier to go up than to come down. We teased him about that when we came to the next uphill portion of the trail.

Then the boys discovered the huge snowbanks that were suddenly all around us. The sun was blazing down, and with the high reflectivity of the snow, we paused to lather up with some suntan lotion. Hats were cinched down, and sunglasses were made mandatory. Everyone had a great time, even the dog who went berserk with snow in August! But then as the sun dropped lower in the sky, a breeze came up, and a few clouds started to form. It was time to head for our evening destination, Lower Jean Lake. It is somehow very relaxing to only have to worry about the simplest things—looking at the sky to check on the weather now and then, keeping aware of how low the sun is getting in the sky so as not to be too late in finding a spot for the night, counting how many fish have been caught and figuring out what to eat with them. You feel like you are getting back to the basics of life, of living, of merging with natural things, of putting yourself into perspective. We really are very small in comparison with such grand surroundings.

We arrived at Lower Jean Lake within the hour. All of the activity on the rocks and snowbanks only seemed to refresh the boys. They led the way, but always in sight. We set up our tent on rocky, but level ground. Out came the Svea stove and within ten minutes hot soup was ready. The timing was just right, for a chilly wind started to blow over the snowfields. Everyone had their down shirts on by 5:00 P.M. By 7:00 Greg and Chris were ready to hit the sack.

The next morning we headed for Elbow Lake, perched nearly 11,000 feet high and overlooking the entire Wind River Range. This was to be our deepest penetration into the

Scene of Jean Lakes with Wind River crest in background.

Greg and Chris take quickly to the high barren country above treeline. Here they have scaled a “mountain” below the crest of the range.

Bridger Wilderness, approximately sixteen miles from our starting point. We had not seen another person for two full days. The only wildlife were the ever-present marmots sending their whistles back and forth across the rocks.

We spent the afternoon exploring around the shoreline of Elbow Lake and trying to catch the golden trout that the lake was reportedly known for. The fish were there, but it was not Jim's day to catch them. We settled for a freeze-dried evening meal as we watched the sun set on the rocky peaks around us. Our initial feelings of apprehension about this barren land had completely disappeared. We felt strangely at peace with this environment.

Although thunderstorms skirted us during the night, the morning was clear again. We started back for Upper Jean Lake. It got so hot that we all took a brief dip in the frigid water. Jim made up for getting skunked the day before by catching eight fish in a hour and a half while Ann and the boys sunbathed and waded at the edge of the lake.

When we got back to Fremont Crossing we decided to take a short cut to Island Lake. This was prompted by the appearance of two backpackers who had come down Fremont Creek from Island Lake. The trail was elusive, appearing in places to be a game trail at best, but even though it was not on our map (it is on a more current version) there was no worry; we could see that there were only about two miles to the lake. All we had to do was follow the creek upstream. About halfway along we found a pleasant campsite a safe distance from the stream. It was already 5:00 P.M. Being off the main trail, we had the woods entirely to ourselves.

The next day was probably the most rigorous of the trip. It started out easily with a mile trek over gentle terrain to spectacular Island Lake. It lived up to all our expectations. It was like a precious jewel situated there at the base of towering Fremont Peak. Lovely waterfalls interrupted the shoreline where streams cascaded down from Titcomb Lakes.

After lunch we tackled the steep climb out of Island Lake to the turnoff for Lester Pass. That was to be a long arduous

Spectacular Island Lake is a favorite camping area for rock climbers who scale the highest peaks in Wyoming.

climb to an elevation of 11,560 feet, the highest point we reached on all of our trips. By this time the boys were used to hiking, were well adjusted to the higher elevations, and were really pleased with their ability to hike with us. We had to make numerous stops on this climb, both for water and for the customary lemon drops. We were really amazed how well the boys did. They just climbed right up the mountain. They got a real thrill out of reaching the signpost at the summit before we did.

It turned out that the descent of Lester Pass was to be equally challenging to our young backpackers. The south side had a huge snowbank that plunged away out of sight from the top. It was too big to walk around and too steep for an obviously safe crossing. Jim carefully went first, stamping deep boot steps into the snow. This proved tricky on the steepest portion because there the runoff from the previous day had frozen to a hard rind. A slip at this point would have meant a painful landing on the talus below. Jim backtracked and tried another route which turned out to be softer and much safer.

Our seventh campsite of the trip was at Lake Nelson, nestled in the south slope of the mountain. Jim had the rest of the afternoon to try again for golden trout. This time he successfully caught four nice ones. Meanwhile the boys and Ann hiked partway around the lake and up a ridge where the Cook Lakes were visible a few miles to the south. Even the boys seemed to sense that feeling of power one gets when on a high point surveying the country for miles around. It is a feeling that can never be experienced in flatter country. Those moments spent at the summit are exhilarating and uplifting.

By morning it was very calm, which caused swarms of mosquitoes to come out. We bundled up the boys with long sleeves and repellent and packed up in a hurry. We had mixed feelings leaving the high country. When we first got above timberline we missed the security the trees gave. Then we grew used to the grand vistas and came to regard the trees as confining.

The boys enjoyed fishing with Jim at the Cook Lakes. After two hours they had caught nine brook trout. We had to think of making some progress back to the car. Even with all the fish we were eating, the food was getting low. The country became more subdued and less interesting. It got lumpy and rocky and seemed to go up and down and nowhere in particular—a real anticlimax after the high country. Again the lakes did not look like the ones on the map. We had gotten off onto a secondary trail once more. It was going west, however, and parallel to the large stream that drained Cook Lakes. After the strenuous climbs of the day before, the children were understandably tired, so we found a campsite along an unnamed pond, which we christened "Leech Pond" in honor of its inhabitants. It was cloudy and dark. A coyote broke the night's stillness with its plaintive howl.

On the ninth day we started thinking about how nice it would be to get back to the car. The scenery was still not particularly interesting. The children dawdled. We had to think of new games to get them moving. We finally got back on the main trail by late afternoon and camped at Ecklund Lake which is the one next to Barbara. We were almost back! After a late afternoon thundershower a real swim in warmer Ecklund Lake felt wonderful. It had been several days since the dip in Jean Lake, and that was so brief as to hardly count as a swim.

We found it much easier and quicker packing out the next day than it had been packing in on the first day. Now it was downhill, and our food was almost gone, making the packs much lighter. It was a clear day. Many parties passed us on their way in, looking with surprise at the boys, now seasoned veterans of the trail. We reached the trailhead parking lot about 2:00. Everyone was glad to be back. After ten days we were hungry for fresh fruit and vegetables. After a quick trip into town we returned to Fremont Lake for a refreshing swim.

It seemed impossible that we had hiked close to 100 miles with the boys that summer. That afternoon, for the first time since we had started hiking back at Green River Lake, both boys had a long nap. They were never interested in a nap on the trail. They were too busy climbing rocks, running down the trail, catching fish, and having fun. It was a well-earned nap!

10
Looking Ahead

IN AN ATTEMPT to draw together what has been said in these preceding chapters, Bob Marshall's image of the wilderness as a vanishing snowbank on a south-facing slope vividly returns. The wilderness and primitive areas, the national parks, and other federal lands represent the last vestiges of our natural environment as it was before man came on the scene. It is rather incredible the impact man has had on a once ecologically stable environment. With his insatiable appetite for energy, man has learned to shape his environment to his own needs. In so doing, he has momentarily increased his material good but at the expense of nonmaterial values. As the energy crisis becomes a reality and our natural fuels become even more depleted, we are in danger of losing one of our greatest nonrenewable resources—wilderness.

There is yet another change, perhaps more subtle in nature, that is symbolized in our minds by the vanishing snowbank. That is the change in the wilderness experience itself. We have little doubt that our present wilderness areas will materially survive, but the fundamental experience we derive from them may not. Continued abuse of many back-

This is the intangible part of the wilderness experience. It has become a family experience to us.

country regions has already led to changes none of us want to see. Controlled access and wilderness-use controls are already in effect in parts of California's high Sierras. Restrictions on the number of people permitted in more popular areas during periods of heavy use are being imposed. There are advance reservations and even waiting lists. Unfortunate as it is, such measures are unavoidable until the careless backpacker changes his ways. As the necessity for protecting the environment in this manner increases, the personal value of the wilderness experience is endangered simply because we may end up imposing the very qualities on an area we are trying to get away from in the first place.

Looking ahead, the common objective of all dedicated backcountry travelers must be the preservation of the wilderness experience. This means that every person must adhere to a strict wilderness ethic, and be uncompromising toward others who have less regard for the values at stake. In this respect, the romanticism of our pioneering forefathers has no place in a modern ethic. The days of the woodsman who carved his home in the wild are gone. In its place, modern technology, ironically enough, has provided the means by which a family may enter the wilderness, remain there for several days, and return without leaving a trace of their presence. Lightweight pack frames, tents, sleeping bags, stoves, and the like make this possible, and eliminate all need for relying on the material resources of the environment. It is only in this way that the fundamental ingredients of the wilderness experience will be preserved.

We have attempted in the preceding chapters to relate some of our own philosophy of backcountry behavior we believe is essential to the preservation of the wilderness experience. In particular, we have tried to convey how small children can participate and even contribute to this end. It is well and good to complete a successful backpacking trip with children. The personal and family satisfactions derived from these experiences have immense value, at least to us. But in our minds there is more to a successful backpacking trip than these aspects alone. A totally successful trip for us is one in which we have taken the extra time and effort to not only eradicate all signs of our presence but to gather up someone else's garbage as well.

It is important that children (and adults) willingly participate in cleanup and conservation activities. They can do the job because they are told to, but the proper motivation must have one key ingredient. That is, one has to simply care. Greg and Chris may never be ardent conservationists, but hopefully they will grow up caring about what is happening to the environment around them. It really does not matter whether the environment is your backyard, a city park, or an alpine meadow. If one cares enough about it and recognizes that it has value for its own sake, then it will be preserved. Everyone has seen the child who thoughtlessly tosses a candy wrapper or soft drink can into the street, or adults, for that matter, who deface trees and rocks for no apparent reason. These acts, for the most part, do not reflect any particular malice, but rather ignorance of the long-term consequences of such behavior. It often boils down to the fact that many people simply don't care, one way or the other. An apathetic view of the environment, particularly of wilderness areas, can potentially destroy the wilderness experience.

The most effective way to instill these concepts in the minds of small children is by example. If your behavior as parents or group leaders is in tune with a good wilderness ethic, then the chances are good that your followers will behave accordingly. The ethic we have developed, and to which we are personally dedicated, is impossible to formulate entirely on paper because of the intangible aspects. The tangible parts, however, have all been covered in one form or another in this book. They are summarized here as a guide for wilderness behavior.

1. Always camp in small groups.
2. Camp at a single site for no longer than one or two nights.

3. Always camp a respectable distance from water sources.
4. Build campfires only when necessary and when there is a surplus of dead wood.
5. Set each new campsite in order when you arrive, and leave with the satisfaction that no evidence remains of your stay.
6. Avoid littering trails and pick up after those who do.
7. Stay on established trails rather than cut across switchbacks.
8. Treat wild plants and animals with respect.
9. Avoid loud noises in keeping with nature's way.
10. Pack everything out you pack in.

That pretty well sums it up. In our minds the extra effort it takes to adhere to this ethic is a small price to pay in view of the values at stake. It is our hope that our children and yours will learn it well.

Have a good trip!

For Further Reading

America's Backpacking Book, Raymond Bridge, Scribner's, New York, 1973. Several pages on how to incorporate children in backpacking activities.

Backpacking, Robert C. Rethmel, Burgess Publishing Co., Minneapolis, 1974. Fifth edition contains new chapter on backpacking with children.

Backpacking for Fun, Thomas Winnett, Wilderness Press, Berkeley, 1972. His very good chapter "Taking Children" has tips for equipment, food, trail, and camp situations.

Backpacking, One Step at a Time, Harvey Manning, R. E. I. Press, Seattle, 1972. Besides being an excellent text on all aspects of backpacking, the chapter "Suffer the Little Children" gives several hints how to keep young ones moving on the trail and gives chronological age suggestions for how much should be carried.

Coping with Crib Size Campers, Lucille W. Trost, Stackpole Books, Harrisburg, Pa., 1968. This book is especially good for car-camping with infants and also has one chapter, "Infant Camping in the Backcountry," that tells how to keep baby happy in backpacking situations.

The Family Camping Guide, James and Barbara Newman, World Publishing Co., Cleveland and New York, 1967. This is a good primer on basic camping with children with a good chapter on car travel tips and a small chapter on backpacking.

The Family Wilderness Handbook, Mary Scott Welch, Ballantine Books, New York, 1973. Her chapter "And Take the Children" emphasizes slowing down and gives suggestions for children's gear. She also suggests relaxing standards of cleanliness so that everyone can have a good time.

Going Light with Backpack or Burro, The Sierra Club, edited by David Brower, 1968. Chapter 13, "Children," has helpful food and equipment suggestions for young children including security items for the very young.

The Hiker's and Backpacker's Handbook, Bill Merrill, Winchester Press, 1971. Good pointers about hazards to watch for with children are to be found in a section in Chapter 3 entitled "Basic Rules." He also has general trailside and camp tips in taking children.

Pleasure Packing, Robert S. Wood, Condor Books, Berkeley, 1972. "Family Trips" is a helpful chapter telling how to know the area you will be taking children and to gear the trip toward their interests. He also has good tips for keeping children interested on the trail.

The Sierra Club Wilderness Handbook, The Sierra Club, edited by David Brower, Ballantine Books, N.Y., 1968. Chapter on "Children" identical to that found in *Going Light with Backpack or Burro*.

Walking in the Wild, Robert J. Kelsey, Funk & Wagnalls, N.Y., 1974. Scattered references throughout dealing with equipment and situations with children including a nice introduction on reasons for starting children early.

Index